If you think God retired after the New Testament, read a few of these testimonies! In this series, Melanie Hemry and Gina Lynnes share the true stories of believers, just like you, who have run into all kinds of tragedies and come out on the winning side—and their amazing testimonies will show you that miracles are still happening today!

Melanie Hemry is a gifted writer whom I've known for many years. She co-authored this series because she knows, like I do, that anyone who has the gall and audacity to *obey* and *believe* God's Word can see His power in his or her life.

To me, the anointing *is* power—because you can't have healing without it. You can't receive a miracle without it, you can't get saved without it, and you can't experience divine protection without it! The anointing is God's presence rubbing off on us. He is the Power Source, and His anointing isn't just for holy men; it's for any believer who will reach out in faith, obedience, and sincerity to Him—including you.

God bless you as you read and may God's amazing energy and power flow through you!

—Dr. Jesse Duplantis
Jesse Duplantis Ministries

Jesus said if you know the truth, the truth will set you free. In this book, Melanie and Gina have presented the truth in a way that makes it fun and easy to understand. Their stories will fill you with faith, hope, and love. So get comfortable and prepare to receive the anointing that will destroy every yoke and remove every burden in your life.

—Mylon and Christi Le Fevre
Mylon Le Fevre Ministries

I have been associated with Gina for many years. What a teacher, what an author, what a friend. A great man of God spoke by the Spirit of God that in the last days, people would so understand the Word of God that it would be like a formula. This book is the "how to." It has much teaching through wonderful testimonies as well as impartations. I truly love it...it's a must for your faith library.

—Lynne Hammond

ANOINTING for LOVED ONES' SALVATION

By Melanie Hemry
and Gina Lynnes

WHITAKER
HOUSE

ANOINTING FOR LOVED ONES' SALVATION

ISBN: 978-0-88368-688-1
Printed in the United States of America
© 2007 by Melanie Hemry and Gina Lynnes

Whitaker House
1030 Hunt Valley Circle
New Kensington, PA 15068
www.whitakerhouse.com

Library of Congress Cataloging-in-Publication Data

Hemry, Melanie, 1949–
Anointing for loved ones' salvation / by Melanie Hemry and Gina Lynnes
p. cm.
Summary: "Shows the power of the anointing for salvation through real-life stories"—Provided by publisher.
ISBN 978-0-88368-688-1 (hardcover : alk. paper) 1. Anointing of the Holy Spirit. 2. Salvation—Christianity. 3. Holy oils. I. Lynnes, Gina, 1954– II. Title.
BT123.H435 2007
242—dc22   2007033335

1 2 3 4 5 6 7 8 9 **ШJ** 12 11 10 09 08 07

This book contains Rose of Sharon scented oil, representing the spiritual salvation Christ provides us. It reminds us that our heavenly Bridegroom delivers us from the wilderness of sin and brings us into His garden of righteousness.

CONTENTS

"IF YOU ARE EAGER FOR REAL JOY, [I AM] PERSUADED THAT NO JOY OF GROWING WEALTHY, NO JOY OF INCREASING KNOWLEDGE, NO JOY OF INFLUENCE OVER YOUR FELLOW CREATURES, NO JOY OF ANY OTHER SORT, CAN EVER COMPARE WITH THE RAPTURE OF SAVING A SOUL FROM DEATH."

—C. H. SPURGEON

PART ONE

ON THE ROAD TO A MIRACLE

BY GINA

Then Saul, still breathing threats and murder against the disciples of the Lord…came near Damascus, and suddenly a light shone around him from heaven. Then he fell to the ground, and heard a voice saying to him, "Saul, Saul, why are you persecuting Me?" And he said, "Who are You, Lord?" Then the Lord said, "I am Jesus, whom you are persecuting. It is hard for you to kick against the goads." So he, trembling and astonished, said, "Lord, what do You want me to do?"
—Acts 9:1, 3–6

I t's astonishing what almighty God can do with an ordinary road trip.

When Saul of Tarsus strapped on his sandals and trudged down the dusty highway to Damascus muttering threats and hating Christians, he never dreamed he would become one before he arrived. It never occurred to him that on the way, he would be forever changed.

Some two thousand years later when my friend, Danielle Kelley, and I stuffed our suitcases in the trunk of my mud-spattered Nissan, we weren't thinking in those terms either. As we headed down the interstate in the driving rain, we didn't expect anymore than Saul did that someone's eternal destiny was about to be altered. After all, this wasn't a mission trip. It was just a seven-hundred-mile drive from Oklahoma to Colorado and, except for bathroom breaks and an occasional fast-food fix, it would be nonstop.

Unless Danielle snagged some lost soul at a rest stop, she'd have no time for evangelism today. We had too much territory to cover.

I didn't say as much to her, of course. She's one of those fiery Christians who believes God's anointing for salvation can save anybody, anytime, anywhere, and she prays daily along those lines. But, no matter. Apart from a brief *God bless you* to the teenager handing us a sack of hamburgers out a drive-through window, Danielle would have nobody to witness to on this trip but me—and I've been saved for years.

The only other listening ears available to her were attached to the three Yorkshire terriers that curled up in our laps and pressed their noses against the car windows as we rolled across the Kansas plains. Although they were sweet and attentive, they weren't exactly a group that could respond to an altar call.

Then the cell phone rang. Pushing a Yorkie out of the way, Danielle dug into her purse with gusto.

"Yes? Hey, Rich!" she chirped as she clamped the phone to her ear. "Great to hear from you. How are you? Yes… okay…sure….I see. So you're ready now?"

I reached over and pressed the *Stop* button on the CD player so she could hear, and I could eavesdrop, with greater ease. Training my eyes on the black ribbon of asphalt that stretched for miles ahead, I pretended to concentrate on my driving and mind my own business.

"No, Rich, you don't have to be in a church building to do it," Danielle said, shifting her shoulder to steady the puppy that perched there like a parrot, gawking at the Kansas cows whizzing past the window. "We can pray together right now on the phone. Just say, 'Lord Jesus, I receive You now as my Lord and Savior…'"

Outside, the rain rat-a-tatting on the roof eased to a soft mist. I glanced skyward through the windshield to see the sun wrestle its way through steel-gray clouds as if determined to shine on this amazing moment. For an instant, all seemed heavenly, supernatural. *Right now,* I thought, *some precious soul is stepping out of spiritual darkness into the dazzling light of God's love. At this moment, someone is escaping the gaping maw of hell and having his name written in the Lamb's Book of Life. Someone is getting born again.*

Pressing my foot on the gas pedal, I swung into the left lane to pass a lumbering 18-wheeler. The greasy spray of its wake slapped a wave of gunk across my glorious view and brought me back to earth. No pipe organ played hymns for Rich as he gave his heart to Jesus. No pastor knelt with him at a church altar. The only soundtrack was the slap-swoosh of my windshield wipers and the sound of Danielle's New York accent on the cell phone as she led him in prayer:

"Jesus, I believe that You are the divine Son of God; that You died for My sins; that You were crucified, buried, and rose again. I believe that You reign in heaven as the King of kings and Lord of lords. I acknowledge to You that I am a sinner in need of salvation and I ask You to forgive me and save me now. I renounce the devil and all his works in my life. Come into my heart and make me a child of God. I surrender myself spirit, soul, and body to You forever. From this moment on, I am Yours."

Settled back in the right-hand lane, the semi retreating in my rearview mirror, I batted a tear from the corner of my eye, amazed at how God intertwines the miraculous and the mundane. He always hides the spectacular in ordinary surroundings so that only those who are searching can find it. Baby Jesus made His grand entrance in a stable surrounded by hay and farm animals. This man made his entrance into the kingdom of God praying on a cell phone with a blue-jeaned woman surrounded by lap dogs and empty coffee cups.

I cast a sideways glance toward Danielle. The phone still bonded to her ear, her face radiated joy as Rich asked her about reading the Bible and going to church. Her head bobbed up and down as if he could see her nodding in answer to his questions. The motion reminded me of times when I fished off my uncle's dock as a kid and the red and white bobber on my line dipped up and down in the lake, signaling me that I had hooked a perch. Well, Jesus said He'd make us *"fishers of men"* (Matthew 4:19).

I hadn't expected Him to fulfill that promise while we were speeding across the prairie at the maximum limit of seventy miles an hour. But Danielle did. She lived every day expecting to catch souls for Jesus along the highway of life because, like Saul, she once had a road-to-Damascus experience herself. She knows what it's like to climb into a car expecting an uneventful journey and end up meeting Jesus face-to-face.

A Divine Visit with a Teenage Atheist

It happened when she was sixteen. On a normal day like any other, Danielle, her sister Roseanne, and friend Jenny were cruising the streets of East Port, New York, when a dog darted across the road. Jenny's scream split the air. The screech of tires and the explosion of metal curling around an oak tree swallowed up Jenny's voice, and all went silent.

The next morning's light found Danielle unconscious in a hospital bed, swathed in bandages, 150 stitches in her face, with only a fifty-fifty chance of survival—a teenage atheist hovering between life and death.

Danielle hadn't always been an atheist. She'd grown up believing what she'd been taught in her traditional religion: that Jesus was a fearsome Judge, an accuser who looked at her with anger and disapproval. As Danielle understood it, Jesus was the reason the teachers at her parochial school whacked her with rulers and left stinging red welts on her skin. He was the reason they punished her with little mercy for the most minor infractions. Jesus wanted her to be good, or so they said. And it pleased Him for them to use such methods to make her so.

At fourteen, Danielle escaped Jesus the only way she knew how—by proclaiming herself an atheist. But it's hard to stay an atheist when Jesus Himself comes to visit you. And that's what He did as Danielle lay in the stillness of her hospital room, oblivious to the quiet beep of the heart monitor and the shushing of nurses' rubber-soled shoes passing by her door.

He opened His visit with music. Angelic voices, swirling around her in heavenly harmony, lifted Danielle out of her body and into another world. There were no instruments accompanying the angel choir. No harps or violins. Just sweet, melodious voices that embraced her like comforting arms.

When the music stopped, she saw Him. He stood before her, robed in light, His tender eyes resting on her with all-engulfing love. They drew her to Him like a flame draws a moth to its light. One look at Jesus convinced her that she no longer wanted to escape Him. She longed, instead, to spend all of eternity wrapped in His gaze.

Then He spoke. "I love you, Danielle," He said. "Your time has not yet come. Go back and spread the Word."

Danielle didn't want to go back. Life on earth paled like a faded black-and-white photo next to the radiant, Technicolor beauty of Jesus. Why was He making her go back there? And what Word did He want her to spread?

Seven years would pass before Danielle found the answers to those questions. Seven years filled with drugs, pain, and sin. But all that time, God's Holy Spirit was working on her, bringing her to the point of salvation. She resisted Him for a while and tried to shrug off her divine visitation.

One day after smoking a joint, she even went with a friend to the home of a Christian woman, intending to mock her for her faith. Instead of rebuking Danielle, the lady served them tea and kind words. Smitten with conviction, Danielle rushed toward the door. "Jesus loves you," the lady called out after her as she fled the house. "He wants to take that marijuana from you."

Six years later, Danielle finally listened to those words. She had no other choice. Her beautiful, raven-haired daughter was dying from an incurable blood disease. She had nowhere else to turn. So she bought a Bible, took it home, and fell to her knees.

"Jesus, please heal my daughter," she said. Then she surrendered her life to Him.

In an instant, everything was different. Danielle could sense it. She felt clean and light inside. She put her head on the pillow that night, praying that the next morning she would still feel the same.

Sure enough, when dawn crept into her bedroom and nuzzled her to life, she awoke feeling clean and free. She pushed back the curtains and found the sun shining brighter than usual. For the first time ever, she heard birds singing outside her Brooklyn apartment. Best of all, her desire for cigarettes and drugs had vanished. And her daughter was healed.

Danielle has been spreading the Word that Jesus saves ever since.

Exit 58C to Hays, Kansas, streaked past, followed by a sign promising food and gasoline. I listened to the happy patter of Danielle's voice telling Rich how to start his new life. "So you've already bought a Bible? Great!...No, don't just start at the beginning and read through. That can be hard. Start with the Gospel of John. That will help you learn more about Jesus...Yes, and you'll want to go to church...."

Overhead, the sun won the battle with the clouds and sent them scurrying in all directions. The windshield wipers went silent and returned to their beds, their work done. I tapped my fingertips on the warm steering wheel to the rhythm of the song springing up in my heart—an old Baptist hymn from my childhood days. *I have heard the joyful sound, Jesus saves, Jesus saves; spread the tidings all around, Jesus saves, Jesus saves...*

Beside me in the passenger's seat, Danielle once again wove together the practical realities of earth with the glories of the divine. "Well, Rich, the battery on my cell phone is almost dead so I'll have to call you again later. But before I go, tell me how you feel now that you've been born again?"

Danielle had been looking forward to asking Rich that question for two years. That's how long it had been since she first began telling him the good news. That's how long she had waited for the anointing of God to finish its work and get him "ready" to receive Jesus. When she snapped her phone shut and looked at me, her eyes dancing, I knew the answer he gave her, although simple, was what she expected it to be.

"Well?" I asked, knowing she was bursting to tell me.

"He said he feels different. He feels lighter!" she said, clapping her hands in celebration.

Batting at another pesky tear, I turned my eyes back to the road, knowing that angels were rejoicing with us now as we rolled across the sunny, windswept plains. The Great Shepherd had found another lost sheep and lifted him to His shoulders. Another sinner had been gathered into God's fold.

Somewhere a thousand miles away, a believer named Rich was taking his first few steps with Jesus. No doubt, tomorrow morning when he woke up, he would hear the birds sing.

God loves nothing better than saving souls. It's His passion. He will loose the power of heaven itself, work miracles, perform signs and wonders, send angels, even pay personal visits, if necessary, to snatch one sinner out of the devil's hands. He will cloak the rebellious with such suffocating conviction that it sends them running to Him for relief. He will do anything that love will allow in order to bring a lost son or daughter home.

I wonder, sometimes, how we can doubt that, considering the price Jesus has already paid to redeem mankind. But, truth be told, we often do.

As we lie awake in our beds and think of loved ones who seem hell-bent on rejecting Jesus, we are tempted to assume there is nothing more God can do for them. After all, Jesus already shed His blood, paid the price to save them, and sent messengers to deliver the good news. If our friends or family reject that news, we might expect God to shrug His mighty shoulders and turn His attention to other matters, leaving the rebellious and wayward to their own self-imposed destruction.

But that's just not God's style.

When a sinner slams the door in His face, He doesn't forget about him and go looking for something else to do. He starts searching for an intercessor. He sends His mighty Spirit throughout the earth to find somebody who will keep speaking the truth to that person in love, somebody who will pray for them. He scans every church pew and looks behind every open Bible. He searches high and low for somebody bold enough to believe He can win even the most stubborn soul.

Sometimes the only person He can find is a Christian too wet behind the ears to know any better. I was in that condition when He first made a fisher of men out of me. I had just recently committed my life to Jesus, and I was toddling around in spiritual Pampers, immature but overjoyed to be free of the stink of sin. In the few short weeks I'd spent walking with God, I'd been delivered from things I'd struggled against for years. Uncontrollable anger, black bouts of depression, and a two-pack-a-day cigarette addiction had melted away under the power of Jesus' touch like hailstones in the Texas summer heat. Head-over-heels in love with my Savior, I was convinced there was nothing He couldn't do.

The problem was, I had friends—good friends, beloved friends—who didn't want any part of Him, and I couldn't figure out what to do about it.

My long-time buddy Joe, for example, came close to cursing me every time I mentioned Jesus' name. I didn't relish the persecution, either. I hadn't caught onto the concept of rejoicing and being glad about that yet, so when Joe came to visit, I tried to avoid the subject. "What about this weather?" I'd say when he dropped by. "How are things at work?"

But Joe insisted on pestering me with spiritual questions.

"What's changed with you?" he'd say. "In the years I've known you, you've never been this happy. You've never been this peaceful. What's the deal?"

The first time he asked, I replied with vigor, glad for the opportunity to brag about my Redeemer. "I gave my life to Jesus!" I said. "Turned the whole thing over to Him—lock, stock, and barrel. Made Him the Lord of my entire life. When I did, He started saving me, not just from hell in the hereafter but from the hell on earth I've been living in."

I thought Joe might like that answer. I was mistaken.

"Jeeeeesus!" he roared, his face flaring red as his plaid flannel shirt. "Get out of here with that junk about Jesus. People have beat me over the head with Him since I was a kid, telling me He was going to get me for the bad things I've done and send me to hell. That's nothing but religious hogwash, and I don't want to hear it."

I wasn't as loving as the Christian lady Danielle met. I didn't offer to make Joe tea. I puffed up like a blowfish, all prickly and offended. "Get out of here, yourself!" I snapped. "After all, this is my house; and you're the one who asked the question."

When Joe stormed out, I assumed that was the end of the matter. It didn't look like he would ever be interested in getting saved. But God knew better. He loved Joe and knew,

ON THE ROAD TO A MIRACLE

even if I didn't, that the spiritual bobber was wobbling on the waters of salvation. I had a fish on the line.

A few days later as I puttered around the house picking up toys my kids had strewn around the family room, a strange need to pray seized my heart. Somebody was slipping into spiritual darkness. The Holy Spirit in His great love was sounding the alarm. It was the first time God ever tapped me to intercede in prayer for a lost soul, and at first, I was confused.

For no apparent reason, despair swept over me like a chilly ocean wave. *What's happening?* I looked around in confusion, my hands overflowing with doll clothes and action figures. Everything seemed to be fine; yet deep inside, I sensed something terrible—perhaps something terminal—was about to happen.

For a moment, the wave of grief passed. Then an undertow of spiritual darkness swirled around my heart and pulled me toward a place of eternal darkness so deep and inescapable that, once there, I knew I could never return. "Dear Lord, why am I feeling this way? I know I'm born again. I know I'm headed for eternity in heaven!"

"Yes, you are. But there is another who isn't. Pray for him."

I hurried to the walk-in closet in my bedroom—the only quiet place I could find—and fell to my knees, weeping and praying.

For whom?

I didn't know for sure. I just knew that whoever it was, God loved him enough to die for him. The Holy Spirit had me weeping over him like a mother would weep over a drowning child being swept out to sea. With love greater than any I had ever experienced before, God was throwing out the lifeline.

After I prayed a while, the feeling lifted. I felt normal again. I decided not to tell anybody what had happened to me. If I was going crazy, I preferred to do it in the privacy of my own mind.

> WITH LOVE GREATER THAN ANY I HAD EVER EXPERIENCED BEFORE, GOD WAS THROWING OUT THE LIFELINE TO ONE LOST SOUL.

I had the same experience again the next day...and the next...and the next. The last time it happened, a wonderful sense of joy sprung up within me as I finished praying. I knew then that God's mission had been accomplished. Somewhere a soul had been saved.

During those days, Joe had stopped by a time or two, as ornery as ever, asking me about my newfound peace, then getting mad at my answers. Dumping years of resentment on my dining room table, he sat across from me with a cup of coffee and told me about the legalistic religion that had been forced on him as a kid. He had hated church, hated

ON THE ROAD TO A MIRACLE

all the meanness and hypocrisy he experienced there. He'd even grown to hate the name that was associated with it—the name of Jesus.

I listened and felt bad for him. But even so, the fact remained that Jesus had changed my life. Whether Joe liked it or not, that was the truth.

Shortly after my prayer burden lifted, Joe came by again. I sighed when I opened the door and saw him standing there. *Here we go again.* But this time, Joe's shoulders weren't thrown back in defiance. They drooped. He'd been boxing for days with the conviction of the Holy Spirit, and I could see he'd lost the match.

"Okay, there's no way around it," he said, flopping down on the sofa, a defeated man. "I need what you've found. I'll do whatever I have to do to get it."

Still wary, I kept my distance in case he decided to blast me again. "It's simple, Joe. All you have to do is give your whole self to Jesus—spirit, soul, and body. I know you already believe He exists. You've known since you were a kid that He is the Son of God who died for your sins. You just never received Him into your heart as your personal Lord and Savior."

It was not what I'd call a glorious moment. Joe buried his face in his hands like a man just informed by the IRS that he owed back taxes. "Do I have to call Him Jesus?" he asked. "Can't I use some other name?"

I gaped at him, dumbfounded. I wasn't a seminary graduate, but I was Bible-savvy enough to suspect that the whole process of getting born again depended on calling Jesus by His real name. I didn't think it would work to call Him *Jim* or *Ted* or *Buddha*. I said so; and Joe conceded the point.

Then he prayed.

Joe's experience wasn't like Danielle's or Rich's. "I don't feel any different at all," he said when he finished his prayer. "Maybe it didn't work."

"It always works," I assured him. "Jesus said, *'The one who comes to Me I will by no means cast out'* [John 6:37]. So you can take it to the bank that if you came to Jesus, He received you as His own. Feelings or no feelings, you'll never be the same again."

Joe shrugged and took my word for it. From that day forward, his life began to change.

THE FIRE SPREADS

Over the years, I've come to understand why the devil is so terrified of God's anointing for salvation. I know why he fights tooth and nail to keep us from releasing it by sharing the gospel, praying, and believing for people to be saved. The anointing for salvation is contagious. Once it's turned loose, it spreads from one person to another, bringing even the most unlikely loved ones into the Father's house.

That's what happened with Joe. Once he got cured of his allergy to Jesus' name, he started telling everybody about Him. The first person he told was his nephew, Floyd.

"I hope you don't mind," Joe said one night as he tramped into my house to attend the little Thursday night Bible study a few of us had started. "I invited Floyd to join us. I've been talking to him about the Lord, and he wanted to hear more. I figured this would be a good place for him to do that."

A few minutes later, Floyd arrived. His blue eyes were dilated as big as Frisbees, his long, pale wisps of hair floating about his head in defiance of gravity. His tie-dyed shirt and untied work boots spoke of a kid who had lived on drugs for a long time and was comfortable with it. Instead of a Bible, he carried a six-pack of beer tucked under his arm. "This the Jesus study group?" he asked.

Words escaped me. Opening the door wide enough to accommodate both his skinny frame and his beer cans, I smiled and nodded to welcome him.

The whole Bible study group loved Floyd from the start. We couldn't help it. Never mind that he arrived looking like a strung-out hippy arriving fifteen years late for Woodstock. Never mind that when we asked him even the simplest question, he closed his eyes and meditated for fifteen seconds before he answered because he had to listen to the voice inside his head that told him what to say. We just knew there was something inexplicably precious about Floyd. Jesus loved him, and so did we.

THE ANOINTING FOR SALVATION IS CONTAGIOUS. IT SPREADS LIKE WILDFIRE TO BRING THE MOST UNLIKELY SOULS INTO THE HOUSE OF THE LORD.

Within a few weeks, Floyd gave his life to the Lord. Shortly thereafter, the drugs and the beer disappeared. With a little prayerful help from his friends, so did the voices in his head. He joined a neighborhood church, and though it's still hard for me to picture him standing amid a loft full of cherubic singers dressed in matching polyester robes, last I heard, he'd become one of the most gleeful members of the church choir—long hair and all.

Once Floyd was in the fold, the anointing for salvation leapt like the flames of a forest fire to another surprising soul: my sister's neighbor, Barbara. Much like Joe, Barbara was hostile to Christianity. When it came to other paths to

ON THE ROAD TO A MIRACLE

God, however, her mind was as open as a bat-infested belfry. A New Age devotee, she was steeped in Eastern mysticism. She worshipped a guru named Maharaji who proclaimed himself to be the Perfect Master of his time, just as Buddha was the Perfect Master of his day, and Jesus the Perfect Master of His day.

Barbara meditated on Maharaji for hours, hoping to achieve astral projection. She also studied and believed the predictions of Nostradamus. Convinced his predictions of global catastrophe were imminent, she prepared for them by stashing three thousand dollars' worth of survival rations in her garage.

Demonic spirits of every kind felt welcome in Barbara's house, and a number liked it so well they moved in. As a result, sometimes the lights in Barbara's house blinked on and off for no apparent reason. Her electric toothbrush often whirred of its own free will. On occasion, when Barbara sat cross-legged in her darkened closet, chanting, "Ommm…," she ended up slithering around the floor like a snake. She wasn't sure why those things happened or whether they should concern her. All she knew was that despite her chanting and slithering, something in her spirit still hungered for a more intimate knowledge of God.

In the weeks before she met my sister, Susan, that inner hunger began to express itself in a song she found herself singing in times of meditation, a spontaneous song that rose from her heart. "Dear Lord, I need to know Your name…"

she said, her voice rising and falling in an unfamiliar melody. "I need to know Your name."

When Susan first encountered Barbara, she wondered how she could ever introduce her to Jesus. Barbara had chucked Christianity long ago. Although she'd grown up going to church and had a praying grandmother, once she came of age she discarded her belief in Jesus like an outgrown, moth-eaten coat. The very mention of it irritated her. She had no time for such silliness now that she had a more sophisticated spiritual perspective.

One day in conversation, however, Susan broached the subject without meaning to. She mentioned to Barbara, quite by accident, that Jesus had spoken to her heart about some minor matter in her life.

"What?" Barbara said, her eyebrows jumping toward her hairline like a pair of startled jackrabbits. "JESUS spoke to you? Is that what you just said?"

Stumbling over her words as she tried to explain, Susan broke what to Barbara was the most shocking news. Jesus is alive today. He lives in the hearts of those who make Him their Lord, and speaks to them in a way they can hear Him. Barbara pondered the possibility…then shrugged it off. She had Maharaji to help her and be her guide. Even if Jesus was alive, she wasn't interested in Him.

Jesus, however, was interested in her in a very big way.

ON THE ROAD TO A MIRACLE

Over the next few days, Susan's heart quickened with desire to see Barbara born again, and she prayed with passion for her salvation. On Sunday, Susan went to church as usual. As she stood in the church service, hands raised in worship to God, she experienced a peculiar shift in perspective. She felt as though she had become Barbara, as if she were worshipping the Lord in Barbara's place.

> YOU CAN CARRY LOST SOULS TO THE FATHER BY STANDING IN THE GAP FOR THEM, WHICH IS TRUE INTERCESSION.

Tears twirled down her cheeks as she experienced the joy her lost neighbor would feel at stepping out of the spiritual shadows and into Jesus' light. She wondered what it could mean. Then Holy Spirit spoke to her heart.

"Thank you for bringing Barbara to church with you."

"But, Lord," she argued, "I didn't bring her."

"Yes, you did. You took her place by carrying her in your heart. You stood in for her so that I could reach her. That's called intercession."

The next Saturday night, Susan's phone rang.

"Are you going to church tomorrow morning?" Barbara asked. "If you are, I want to go along."

After her first visit to church, Barbara decided she would give Jesus a kind of trial run. She would take Him on as a second guru for a while, seek His advice and see how things panned out. It didn't go well. She showed up at my sister's door a few days later, frustrated and spoiling for a spiritual fight.

"Jesus won't talk to me like He talks to you!" she chafed.

"I know," Susan answered. "I was praying for you this week, and the Lord told me He wasn't willing to share you with another guru. He can't allow you to just add Him to your growing list of *lords*. He wants to be your only God."

"You mean I have to renounce Maharaji?" Barbara's eyes sparked with fury. "How can I be sure Jesus said that to you? How do I know that you're not the devil trying to take Maharaji away from me?"

Susan's jaw dropped at the question. She'd been accused of a few things in her time—being a less than attentive driver, for instance—but nobody had ever before suggested she might be the devil incarnate.

"Well...uh...all I can tell you is that I'm sure I'm not the devil. You'll just have to trust me on that, I guess."

Barbara let the door slam behind her on the way out.

When a natural baby is born, nobody expects the process to be neat and tidy. Hours of gut-wrenching labor, sweat, a bellow or two (or twenty) from a mom weary of the whole ordeal, and bodily fluids galore are just part of the package. We know that. But when it comes to delivering spiritual babies, we cling to the hope that some angelic stork will deliver them, that they will arrive—instantly and with no effort on our part—like little surprises on our church doorstep, all clean, cute, and cuddly.

In reality, spiritual birth, like natural birth, progresses through stages. The seed of God is planted. Prayer waters the seed and helps it grow. Then labor starts and things get uncomfortable, even painful at times. That was especially true for Barbara. When the pain set in, she quit communicating for a few days.

Uncertain if Barbara would welcome a call from someone she suspected to be the devil, Susan hesitated to initiate contact. Then one day the Lord spoke an enigmatic phrase to her heart.

"Take Barbara a birthday card today."

Had she heard right? She picked up the phone and dialed Barbara's number.

"Hi, Barb, it's Susan. Is it your birthday today?"

A cacophony of gulps, sobs, and snuffles erupted in response to the question. Pressing the receiver to her ear trying to decipher the code, Susan heard the whisk of a tissue being freed from a cardboard box. "I suppose you could say it is," Barbara answered, blowing her nose. "I gave my life to Jesus today. I got what you call born again.

But I think I spent so long in the birth canal I came out with a pointed head!"

With that, the two new spiritual sisters, now part of the same divine family, burst into gales of laughter as refreshing as the first breezes of spring. Barbara didn't just feel different. She felt revolutionized. She felt re-created; and, indeed, she was.

Within days, God's anointing for salvation spilled over from Barbara's life into the life of her troubled nine-year-old daughter, Heather, who was suffering from the spiritual darkness that had once flooded their home. Beset with fears, demonic torments, and behavior problems, Heather listened, intent, as Susan told her how to receive Jesus as her Savior. "He loves you and will make you feel safe," Susan explained.

Heather prayed and gave her heart to the Lord. She became a different child from that moment on.

In time, Barbara's mother was born again too. And her sister. And some friends who had once been fellow Marharaji worshippers. And the list goes on.

More than twenty years have passed since Barbara was born, pointy-headed, into the kingdom of God. Looking at her now, it's hard to believe she's the same woman who once had no interest in Jesus. These days she is a woman aglow with life and love for the Lord and for others. She still goes to the church where my sister once interceded for her in prayer and worship. When the praise music begins, she is the first to lift her hands in honor to the Lord. Nobody has to take her place.

Almost all my friends were born again within the first few months of my walk with the Lord. After that, I'm embarrassed to admit, I laid my spiritual fishing pole aside. I didn't think much about the fact that there were other people who needed Jesus—people He loved just as much as He loved me and my little circle of acquaintances. Since I worked at a Christian ministry and spent most of my free time at church, I lived ensconced in a cocoon of Christians. If perchance I did stumble into an inadvertent conversation with a lost person, I got tongue-tied. I couldn't find the right thing to say.

Now and then, after a hearing a sermon at church about the Great Commission, I did consider hurling myself toward some poor, lost soul in a desperate attempt to witness to them. Driven by guilt, I'd work to figure out how I could slip a mention of Jesus into the brief exchange I had with the cashier at the grocery store, for example.

"Lettuce, twenty-five cents a pound," she'd say. "Newspaper, fifty cents."

Speaking of newspapers, have you heard the good news about Jesus? I'd imagine replying in response. But I could never get the guts to do it. The very thought felt contrived and forced. I envisioned the irritated cashier clubbing me with the lettuce head to shut me up, and my resolve to witness wilted.

How shameful! I'd think to myself. *I am too timid to tell lost people about Jesus.* Walking across the parking lot to my car, my plastic grocery sack dangling beside me, flogging my knees as if to punish me for my failure, I would wonder how to fix my problem.

One morning as I read my Bible, a solution emerged. I read that Jesus said to His disciples when He sent them out to preach the gospel, *"The harvest truly is plentiful, but the laborers are few. Therefore pray the Lord of the harvest to **send out** laborers into His harvest"* (Matthew 9:37–38, emphasis added). Grabbing my Bible dictionary, I looked up the word *"send"* and learned it is translated from the Greek word *ekballo*. It means "to eject, bring forth, cast (forth, out), drive (out), expel, or thrust out."

"Heavenly Father," I prayed. "This is what I need! I need to You to eject me out of my timidity and thrust me into the harvest field. I need You to drive me out there with Your supernatural power."

If you think God won't do that, think again. Not only will He answer that prayer, He'll do it without warning you in advance. One day, in the midst of a seemingly ordinary activity, He'll strap a spiritual rocket launcher to your back, and you'll find yourself saying things by the power of His Spirit that you never intended to say.

I found that out a few weeks later. During my morning devotions, I sensed the Lord prompting me to call a particular beauty salon and make an appointment to get my nails done. *Wow, that's strange! Why would the Lord all of a sudden be so interested in my fingernails? And why would He want me to go to the most expensive salon?* Whatever the reason, I was happy to obey the leading and wished for more along the same line.

At the salon I seated myself in front of Debbie, the nail technician, and smiled at her. *How nice to be in the center of God's will.* We introduced ourselves to each other and small talked for a while. When the conversation waned, I squinted my eyes and tried to read the article titles on the magazines stacked in a rack across the room. Content to sit in silence, I listened to the hum of blow driers and the murmur of women's voices mixing with the scritch-scritch of the file against my nails. The sun baked the air as it streamed through the plate-glass window around black, stenciled letters advertising a list of beauty services and declaring *Walk-ins Welcome.*

I stifled a yawn. If I didn't make conversation, I was going to slide out of my chair and end up dozing on the floor.

"Well, Debbie," I said, "How has your day been today?"

Without my realizing it, the rocket launcher had been activated. The countdown began. I had just been thrust into the harvest field.

Debbie didn't look up. She bent over my hands and concentrated on clipping my cuticles as if she were a surgeon removing a brain tumor. Then a tear splashed past the clippers and onto the table.

"Are you all right?" I asked.

More clipping.

"Debbie?"

She lifted her head and met my gaze with eyes swimming in sorrow. She swallowed hard and struggled to reign in her emotions so she could speak. "My husband left me this morning," she said. "Without warning, he walked into the kitchen while I was fixing our son's breakfast and, suitcase in hand, he said he didn't want to be married to me anymore. Then he walked out."

I hesitated, searching my heart for an appropriate response. "Oh, Debbie, I'm so sorry. You must be crushed." I thought again about what she'd said. "Are you saying you had no marriage problems until this morning?" I asked, sure I had misunderstood her.

Dropping the clippers, she buried her face in her hands and yielded to a flood of grief. "Yes, that's what I'm saying!" she sobbed, her shoulders shaking. "We never fought. We had a good marriage. He's always been my best friend. He's a good father. He never said anything about being unhappy. I have no idea what happened."

I wanted to comfort her but had no clue how. I looked for a leading from the Lord. Surely, in this situation, He would give me something spiritual to say.

"Tell her that her husband left her because he's gotten trapped in homosexuality. He's involved with another man."

I froze as the words registered on my heart. *No way! There is no way I am going to say that to this woman. What if I'm wrong?*

Even if I'm right and this is a supernatural word of knowledge, how is it going to comfort her? Please, Lord, if You really want me to do this, give me some confirmation that I'm on the right track.

"Debbie," I said hoping she didn't notice the quiver in my voice. "Have you noticed anything unusual in his behavior lately? Anything at all?"

"Just that he wanted to get away by himself for a little vacation a few weeks ago. He said he'd been so busy at work that he needed a day or two alone. So he spent a weekend in Cancun. He's never done that before."

"He went alone?"

"Well, not totally," Debbie said, dabbing at mascara-smudged eyes. "A guy he knows from work went with him."

So that was it. I had heard the Lord correctly. Compassion for Debbie swept over me. I didn't care if she threw the clippers at me when I said it. I didn't care if she threw the whole table. This time, I would open my mouth and obey the Lord.

Debbie stared at me, stunned, when I told her. She stopped crying and drew a startled breath as the pieces of the puzzle came together. Events, clues she'd seen and overlooked clicked into place, and she realized it was true.

"How did you know?" she whispered. "You've never even met my husband. How could you possibly have guessed?"

That's when I told her about Jesus. How He loves her and wants to help her. How He has good plans for her life. And how He speaks to the hearts of those who know Him and listen to His voice.

I didn't lead Debbie to the Lord that day. It wasn't time. I just planted the seed of the Word and then, week after week, as I came to get my nails done, I watered it by loving her and sharing with her what life with Jesus is like. Unlike Joe and Barbara, Debbie was hungry to hear about Christianity. The whole concept was new to her. She'd never read the Bible. She'd been to church only a few times in her life.

Every time I came into the salon, sat down in front of her, and presented my nails for maintenance and repair, she was brimming with curious questions about the Christian life. She thought my answers were fascinating—not because my words were smart, but because the anointing for salvation was on them.

As the months passed, I witnessed the growth process Jesus described in His message about the farmer who plants the Word. There, He said:

> *The kingdom of God is as if a man should scatter seed on the ground, and should sleep by night and rise by day, and the seed should sprout and grow, he himself does not know how. For the earth yields crops by itself: first the blade, then the head, after that the full grain in the head. But when the grain ripens, immediately he puts in the sickle, because the harvest has come.* (Mark 4:26–29)

Sometimes God sends one person to plant the seed of the Word, calls another person to water it with encouragement and prayer, and another to reap harvest. With Debbie, I had the privilege of seeing her through every stage. One day, a few months after her husband walked out, I realized the grain had ripened. Debbie was ready to be born again.

"Hey, I want to ask you about something," she said, swabbing my nails with a cotton ball pungent with polish remover. "Since you're always talking about how Jesus speaks to you, I decided to see if I can hear Him too. I've been listening all week, and I haven't heard a thing. What's the deal with that?"

My heart quickened and I breathed a silent prayer. *Oh God, please don't let me mess this up.*

"Before you can hear Him, you have to make a connection with Him," I answered. "You know, like when you're talking to someone on the phone. The problem is you're disconnected."

Leaning forward, she puffed her cheeks and blew away some file dust that had crept onto my fingernails. "Why am I disconnected?" she asked.

"Because of sin. You know the story of Adam and Eve, right?" Debbie's furrowed brow indicated she wasn't clear on the details of the garden of Eden debacle. I sketched it out for her as briefly as possible.

"Well…Adam and Eve once had perfect fellowship with God. They walked and talked with Him every day. But then they sinned and disobeyed Him. When they did that, they lost their connection to Him. Sin cut them off from Him. Since Adam and Eve are the parents of the whole human race, when they disconnected from God, we all got disconnected. The Bible says it this way, *'All have sinned and fall short of the glory of God'* [Romans 3:23]."

Debbie frowned and pursed her lips. "Well, I'm no sinner," she announced. "I'm a very good person."

Lord have mercy. She had stumped me.

I'd never met anyone who thought they'd never sinned. I thanked God for a moment's reprieve as Debbie exchanged greetings with a customer who pranced past, patting her coiffure and trailing the scent of hairspray. "Looks great, hon!" Debbie gushed. "The highlights are perfect."

She looked back at me. "Now, what were we saying? Oh, right…I was telling you that I'm not a sinner. So why am I disconnected?"

I opened my mouth in blind faith, curious to hear what would come out. "You mean you've never murdered anybody, or stolen anything, or done anything really bad like that," I said.

"Yeah. I've always tried to do what's right."

"Okay, but even so, God is perfect love. In His eyes, anything unloving is sin. Have you ever done anything unloving?"

"You mean like when I say I hate my mother-in-law? That's sin?"

I nodded. Debbie dropped her head to avoid my gaze. Biting her lip, she picked up a bottle of nail polish and shook it with unnecessary vigor. "Okay, then. I'm a sinner. Big time. But what do I do about it? How can I get rid of the sin so I can connect to Jesus?"

Bingo. The question I'd been waiting for had finally been asked.

I told Debbie that Jesus had paid the price for sins and that forgiveness was available through His blood. I explained that He would move into her heart and make her all squeaky-clean inside and turn her into a whole new creation if she would receive Him as Lord and Savior. "You and I can pray right now together if you like. You can give your life to Jesus and get connected to Him today."

For a moment, I was impressed with my own boldness. Imagine me—the person once too timid to mention Jesus in the grocery store—about to pray the sinner's prayer amid a salon full of rich women with their hair in foil wraps and their pedicured feet slathered in perfumed lotion! I didn't care who heard me, I would pray with Debbie right here and she would be born again.

We bowed our heads together and I spoke first to lead the way, "Dear Lord Jesus," I said, raising my voice enough to make sure Debbie could hear me over the clamor around us, "I confess to You that I am a sinner...."

What happened next astounded me. Before Debbie could repeat the words, a supernatural silence engulfed the salon. Blow driers stopped. Conversations ended. The jangling phone on the front desk stopped ringing. As the place went still, I could feel dozens of curious ears stretching our way, straining to hear.

For a moment, my boldness failed. Then I realized the anointing for salvation had swept into the place. My confidence surged. *Let them listen if they want. Maybe they'll all get saved!*

I don't know if they did. But I do know that Debbie got what she was after that day. She made her connection with Jesus. She opened the door of her heart so she could talk to Him and hear His voice. Over the next few months when I went to get my nails done, she told me about the church she joined and how much her son enjoyed going with her. She shared how she was able to forgive her husband and pray that someday he would get his life straightened out.

Jesus mended Debbie's heart with amazing speed. The last time I saw her she was bubbling with joy, about to leave her work at the salon and start a new business. She had discovered some of the good plans God has for her life, and she was ready to get started on them.

Every one of us knows people—like Joe, Floyd, Barbara, or Debbie—who need a Damascus road experience. They might be lost family members our heart has ached over for years. They might be beloved friends who have strayed so far from God that we wonder if He can ever reach them. They might be lost neighbors and coworkers who don't seem to have any interest in Jesus at all.

Is it really possible for the Lord to save people like that?

> EVERY ONE OF US KNOWS PEOPLE WHO NEED A DAMASCUS ROAD EXPERIENCE. CAN GOD SAVE THEM? YES! HE'S DONE IT MILLIONS OF TIMES.

Yes. He's done it millions of times. He is an absolute Master at saving the most unlikely souls in the most unlikely ways in the most unlikely places. As we've already seen, when His anointing for salvation sweeps through, a car full of Yorkies, a hospital room, a toy-strewn family room, or a noisy salon can become a place where heaven meets earth. A place where people rebelling against Jesus run smack into Him and fall in love with Him forever just like a rebel named Saul once did.

I've seen it happen. So have countless others.

I look forward to the day in heaven when Melanie and I can meet them all and hear the stories about how Jesus saved them. No doubt, Melanie will want to write them all down and put them in a book. But this side of eternity, such a thing would be impossible. As the apostle John said, *"If they were written one by one, I suppose that even the world itself could not contain the books that would be written"* (John 21:25)

For now we must be content to share with you a handful of amazing experiences—experiences that prove God's anointing for salvation can penetrate hearts hardened by sin and swallowed up in darkness. It can chase down and apprehend souls who have run from Jesus for years. It can remove the blinders of deception and give the lost relatives and friends and neighbors we so dearly love eyes to see the truth of God's amazing grace.

As you read these stores, may your faith be encouraged and your heart stirred afresh about God's power to save the lost. May you be inspired to call out with renewed fervency for laborers to be thrust into the harvest fields. May you say as the prophet Isaiah once said:

Here am I, Lord! Send me.

PART TWO

WHEN GOD COMES TO CALL

BY MELANIE

NIGHT AMBUSH

The torrid night hung black as silt over Vietnam's Da Nang River. Mac Gober slipped away from his Marine patrol escort and took his post undercover in the sweltering heat. Hairs prickling on the back of his neck warned him that he wasn't the only predator skulking through the velvet darkness. Mac's finger, clammy in the humidity, caressed the trigger of his M-14. He imagined firing, then hearing the answering cracks of AKs and the river exploding with the blast of a mine.

Sitting in one position for hours took its toll, but Mac had no choice. Sounds along the river carried and echoed. One twitch, one movement, a single shift of position could signal his presence to the enemy. He dared not slap at the mosquitoes feasting on his flesh or grope for the leeches burrowed into his skin.

The eerie, brooding silence reminded Mac of how alone he was, like a worm on a hook, dangling before the snipers whose goal was to sabotage the fuel depots—and to get him before he got them. Night ambush was a game that depended on every muscle, every sinew, and every nerve ending being alert and poised for action. Here, it was almost impossible to know the enemy. The one stalking him tonight might be plowing rice paddies with water buffalo in the morning. It might be the man shaving his neck with a straight razor in the PX. The person booby-trapping a trail with a homemade

ANOINTING FOR LOVED ONES' SALVATION

bomb could be the compound's laundry woman…or the shoeshine boy.

Mac had never lived among an unknown enemy before. Not that he hadn't stared into hate-filled eyes and seen death reflected in them. He had. Mac had lived with violence and the constant threat of death his whole life. Not in Vietnam; at home.

Mac's mind wandered back to one of the few happy memories of his childhood—his dad, straddling a 1947 Indian motorcycle, driving around the neighborhood with five-year-old Mac snuggled in front, beaming with joy.

Mac had only a handful of such memories, none of them powerful enough to make him forget the countless nights he'd lain in his bed with a pillow over his head, trying to block out his father's drunken rages and his mother's terrified screams.

At sixteen, after two years of muscle-building varsity football, Mac had decided he'd had enough. Looking his father square in the eye with a friend beside him to lend support, he gave the warning, "You're not going to hurt my mother again."

His father had growled and lunged. Locking his hands around Mac's throat, he'd squeezed like a python. Choking and gasping for air, Mac saw hate in his father's eyes while a demented smile splayed across his face.

"Stop, Mr. Gober, you're killing him!" Mac's friend screamed.

Finally, one of his dad's drinking buddies intervened. "The kid's not worth it! Hell, he's not even a man."

That had been one of the last times Mac had seen his father before leaving for Vietnam. It should have left him hoping never to see the man again. Yet, even after a lifetime of abuse and neglect, he'd felt like a land mine exploded in his soul when he got the letter from his mother telling him about his parents' divorce.

A bird fluttered out of a tree, alerting Mac of danger. Pulling his thoughts back to the present, he lifted his M-14.

You just never knew who might want to kill you.

WHEN GOD COMES TO CALL

Mac had been wound tighter than a steel cable for so long that on the flight home from his tour of duty in Vietnam, he felt as though he was coming apart at the seams. He'd been taken out of the war, but war still raged within.

Long months of tension and terror had taken their toll. The backfire of a passing car, an unexpected tap on the shoulder—even the simplest movements or sounds triggered a response. Still leery of being ambushed in the dark, each night Mac walked past the soft bed with its clean sheets and crawled into the safety of the bathtub to sleep.

Mac migrated to a hangout for bikers where alcohol dulled his senses and the camaraderie among the men gave him a sense of family. Drawn by the happiest memory of his childhood, he bought a chopped Harley shovelhead with a metallic candy-apple red gas tank.

Traveling to Tijuana, he bought drugs and ran them up the coast of Mexico for distribution and sales. Drug trafficking was a way to make money and stay stoned at the same time. If Mac wasn't soaring down the interstate on his chopper, he was flying high from the rush of crank. The mind-altering drugs left him unpredictable and paranoid.

Mac and his biker buddies pulled into a truck stop to eat. The waitress, chewing a wad of gum, asked for their orders.

"I'll have a burger and fries and some coffee," Mac said. She just stood there smacking her gum.

"Give me a burger, fries, and coffee," he said, trying again.

Still smacking her gum, she stared at him.

"Listen, I ain't gonna tell you again. I want you to bring me a burger, fries, and some coffee!" Mac ordered, slamming his fist onto the table.

A fellow biker dubbed Ratman intervened. "Hey, Mac, cool it!" he said.

Furious and unyielding, Mac swept the table clean in a shower of broken glass, then jumped up and overturned it. People screamed as he hurled chairs into the mirror behind the counter and dumped tables of hot food.

"Let's get him out of here before the cops come," Ratman ordered. The bikers grabbed Mac and dragged him outside. That night, sitting around a crackling fire, Ratman asked, "Man, what got into you?"

"I ordered three times, and the old bag didn't bring me my food."

"What are you talking about?" Ratman asked. "You never said a word. You just sat there with a stone-cold expression on your face when the waitress asked for your order."

"I ordered three times!" Mac yelled.

"We're telling you like it is, Mac. You never opened your mouth."

"You should have seen yourself today. You were a real maniac."

"Hey, that's it! Mac the Maniac!" Ratman said.

Not even the new name, Mac the Maniac, slowed his drug use. Needing heavier doses and longer rushes, he added cocaine to the mix. He ate it, smoked it, and drank it, but he didn't use the needle. That was one of the few taboos of the biker gang. You couldn't trust a junkie who shot dope, because a junkie's first loyalty was to the needle.

In a little more than a year, Mac's hair had grown to his shoulders and he'd sprouted an enormous, bushy beard. Unbathed and reeking, he played host to bugs who prowled his beard looking for food. In a bar fight with an opponent of mammoth proportions, Mac lost his front teeth. With two eye teeth hanging down like fangs, his sneer sent shivers down the average spine.

"We call him Mac the Maniac," his fellow bikers explained when bystanders gaped. "He'll do the craziest things. Hey, Mac, here's another pack of razor blades for you to eat. Watch this; it'll blow your mind. He's an animal."

Traveling back to Alabama where he was raised, Mac visited his grandparents, who'd offered him the only unconditional love that he'd ever known. His granddad was a simple man with a profound faith in Jesus. Bedridden and paralyzed, he was delighted to see Mac. His grandparents had no idea that the real purpose of his visits was to cultivate the hidden crop of marijuana he was growing on their land.

Unable to keep a steady job, Mac sold more drugs and broke into homes and businesses, stealing things to sell on the black market. All the while his drug-enhanced rage, growing ever stronger, clawed its way through the last frayed threads of control. One day Mac walked into his mother's boyfriend's house. "Why don't you leave this lousy drunk?" he yelled.

"Get out of my house," the man said, raising a double barrel shotgun. Mac karate kicked it out of his hands, then grabbed him by the throat and slammed him into the wall, beating him on the kitchen floor.

"Stop it, Mac!" his mother screamed as he backhanded her to the floor. "Mac, please don't hit me again," she pleaded, running outside. Mac grabbed her hair in a knot and dragged her back into the house.

It was days before he sobered up enough to realize what had happened: *He'd become what he despised in his father.* The realization fueled Mac's self-hatred as well as his addictions. Heading back to California, he picked up where he'd left off—dealing drugs, prostitution, stealing, extortion, and rape.

Sitting around the clubhouse the bikers referred to as their "church," Mac ripped pages from a Bible and used them to roll his joints. Snorting endless lines of cocaine, he started sniffing PCP. When that wasn't enough, he mainlined heroin. His body out of control, unable to balance himself or focus his eyes, Mac couldn't even ride his bike. Filthy and unkempt, he picked spiders off the wall and ate them.

Adding to his problems, he was out of money. When he called his mother to beg for cash, he convinced her he'd use it to buy clothes and look for a job. She bought the lie and agreed to wire what he needed.

Standing in line at the Western Union office, Mac turned heads. His beard twisted in every direction. His scraggly hair grazed his shoulders. His black biker boots, chains, and dark sunglasses were haloed with a city-dump aroma that choked everyone but Mac himself. Men grimaced and looked the other way. Children hid their faces in their mothers' skirts. A white-haired grandmother pressed a handkerchief to her nose to screen the stench. Curling his lips back to reveal his vampire-like sneer, Mac chomped his jaws, threatening to bite.

As his eyes wandered from the offended crowd in the Western Union line, Mac noticed a man walking down the sidewalk handing out flyers. One by one they were tossed aside. Squinting to try to focus his eyes, Mac read, "JUST AS I AM."

I know who I am, Mac thought. *I am the scum of the earth.* He tried to toss the paper aside, but it stuck to his grubby fingers. Flicking it harder, it stuck to his thumb. He shook his hand, but the paper refused to budge. Then the small print came into focus. "There's such a crazy idea today that people have to give up their bad habits before God can accept them.

But God accepts you just as you are." As he read the rest of the flyer, the words pierced his heart.

The simple plan of salvation—Jesus paying the price for every sin Mac had ever committed—was so outrageous that he sobered up for several days. Then God did something to clench the deal. One morning when Mac stumbled into his apartment in the dark hours before dawn, he stood transfixed at the image of Jesus hanging on a cross in the center of the room. Then words cut the silence with such power that a chill rippled down his spine.

"Mac, I love you." Peace unlike anything he'd ever known washed over him.

"Mac, I love you." "How could You love me?" he sobbed. "But, Mac, I *do* love you."

"Mac, I love you." Mac sank to the floor, hot tears coursing down his beard. "How could You love me?" he sobbed.

"But, Mac, I *do* love you."

Was he hallucinating? Having a flashback? "Lord, I don't know if this is real. I've got to know for sure." The room flooded with intense light. In bold letters looking like they'd been branded into the wall, Mac saw the word *GOD*. A holy fear washed over him.

For the first time in his life, Mac knew that God was real and that Jesus had died for his sins. "Oh, God, I'm so sorry for what I've done!" he wailed. "Please don't let me go to hell! Please forgive me!" He prayed for hours until he'd sobbed himself to sleep.

WHEN GOD COMES TO CALL

Joy Comes in the Morning

The next morning when Mac awoke, his eyes were swollen shut from weeping, yet he felt as though an enormous weight of sin had been lifted off of him. Filled with an overwhelming sense of joy, Mac laughed as he talked to God. "I'm so thankful that You saved me!" he said.

Mac felt so happy it seemed he would explode from sheer joy. He wanted to hug someone. He wanted to shout about the goodness of God. As he stepped into the morning sun, the whole world looked new. Had the sky ever been so blue? Had the sun ever shone so bright or the grass so green?

It was Sunday morning! *I'm going to find myself a church!* Mac climbed into his old car and drove until he found a church. They were in the middle of service when Mac stepped inside. You could have heard a pin drop. Mac, grinning wide and doubled-fanged, walked down the aisle, nodding and waving at the stricken faces. Finding a seat on the front row, Mac looked up at the pastor who appeared to be struggling to speak. As soon as the service was over, Mac walked forward and said, "Brother, I'm coming home."

Legacy of Love

None of Mac's biker buddies wanted to hear about Jesus. Giving up drugs and alcohol, Mac got a legitimate job and saved enough money for the trip back to Alabama. The first thing he did was beg his mother's forgiveness. He wrapped her in his burly arms, and they both wept. Next he visited the jewelry store where he'd stolen diamonds. "I want to ask you to forgive me for what I did to you," he said. "If it takes the rest of my life, I'll repay you every dime."

One by one, he made restitution and repented to all those he'd wronged.

Two years after Mac received Jesus, his grandmother asked him to visit the old farmhouse. His granddad had died in his sleep before Mac gave his heart to the Lord.

"You know your granddaddy loved you?" his grandmother asked, squeezing Mac's hand.

"Yes, ma'am, I know that."

"There are some things you don't know," she continued. "Things that I've held in my heart, waiting for the right time to tell you. Every Sunday the men would drive out here after church and sit with your granddaddy and me. Many a time your granddaddy asked them to lift him out of bed and place him in a praying position. They'd bend him on his knees beside the bed and fold his hands together. They'd hold him like that while your granddaddy cried out to God to save you. He went home to be with the Lord calling your name and believing that one day you'd be saved."

Tears of joy streamed down his grandmother's face as Mac wept deep, wrenching sobs, thanking God that someone loved him enough to pray him out of the hell his life had become and into eternal peace with God.

Ten years after giving his life to Jesus, Mac went back to riding the streets on his Harley. This time he rode with the Tribe of Judah, a band of Christian men who have won the hearts of many sin-hardened bikers to Jesus.

> SOMEONE LOVED MAC ENOUGH TO PRAY HIM OUT OF THE HELL HIS LIFE HAD BECOME AND INTO ETERNAL PEACE WITH GOD.

Today Mac and his wife, Sandra, have three grown children. They run Canaan Land Ministries, a seventy-acre refuge for men like Mac, who are broken and desperate to know that their sins have been forgiven.

Mac Gober learned at a young age that you never know who might want to kill you. But during those months of night ambush in Vietnam, he had no way of knowing how much God wanted to save him. While the enemy stalked him along the banks of the Da Nang River, Mac's praying grandfather had been relentless in stalking the powers of darkness that threatened his grandson's life.

Through prayer, Mac's grandfather had been a sniper in God's army.

He defeated the enemy, set the captive free, and opened the way for God to set His own night ambush.

There is no God," Angelika's father said with finality. "I witnessed Hitler's reign of terror firsthand and wept bitter tears over the slaughter of the Jews. If God existed He would never have allowed them to be massacred. After death there is nothing but worms!" Having made his point, he wandered off to be alone. Even though he had moved his family from Germany to Canada, there would be no talk of God in his home, and no church. He would raise his children as atheists, and he wanted them to understand from an early age that there was no absolute truth.

Angelika quaked in her bed after the lights had been turned out. She hated the darkness because it reminded her of death. And after death, all she had to look forward to was...*worms*. Sobbing into her pillow, she cried herself to sleep.

Despite the tears of her childhood, as Angelika grew up, she adopted her father's perspective. She became as certain as he that there was no God; certainly not the God of the Christians, poor fools. Still, she reasoned, somewhere in the world there had to be an absolute truth; otherwise, life would be meaningless. Deep in her heart, she determined to find it.

As an adult, Angelika went to work in a dinner theatre performing murder mysteries that were written and produced by a man named Dirk Van Battum. Dirk was born in Holland before his family migrated to Canada. Unlike Angelika, his mother had sent him to church on occasion and had given him a Bible. Allowing it to gather dust, he'd studied eastern religions such as Baha'i, which celebrates unity and oneness.

Two years after they met, Angelika and Dirk merged their lives and their business interests. Starting their own company, Black Hat Entertainment, they moved to Phoenix, Arizona to produce and perform their plays. After the onset of the Gulf War in 1992, their enterprise fizzled. The American public, wearied by war, wanted lighter entertainment than murder over dinner. Loading up their infant son, Lorne, Dirk and Angelika drove north toward Canada, looking for a new start.

They found it in the little village of Naramata, British Columbia, among blossoming orchards, vineyards, and flowering plants of every kind. This was a place where they could put down their own deep roots and thrive. Because the village was too small for dinner theatre, Dirk and Angelika decided to open a bookstore. They named it Aradia in honor of the moon goddess, Diana.

Angelika sighed with contentment when they opened for business. Hundreds of fat books dealing with truth lined the shelves: Buddhism, Hinduism, the occult, witchcraft, astrology, and numerology. Tarot cards, dream catchers, and native drums lent atmosphere to the incense-filled store. Light shining through the windows shot rainbows off the crystals glistening in the sunlight. In the back room, Dirk made extra money by reading tarot cards. Angelika never remembered being so happy. *There must be an absolute truth somewhere in all these books, and we're going to find it!*

The morning sun lit the cheery bookstore as Angelika opened for business. Her contented smile faded when she saw the tract someone had slipped under the door. In bold letters it read, JESUS LOVES YOU!

Not again! Someone had made a habit of shoving this kind of trash under their door. She and Dirk were in pursuit of truth—not fantasy. Ripping the tract into pieces, she threw it in the trash before greeting her first customer of the day.

THE SEARCH FOR TRUTH

Dirk and Angelika's first foray in search of truth began with the teachings of the Enlightened One—Buddha. Studying every book in the store on the subject, they learned that when Prince Siddhartha Gautama attained his awakening at age thirty-five, he became known as Buddha—a title anyone who learned without a teacher could assume. Believing that there was no God—only enlightenment— Buddha spent forty-five years spreading the truth as he knew it before dying at the age of eighty. Buddhism, Angelika learned, offered no escape from the worms, only the possibility of being awakened from the "sleep of ignorance."

After months of study, Dirk and Angelika admitted that they just didn't find an absolute truth in Buddhism.

The next stop on their search for truth took them to Hinduism. The "eternal law," they discovered, was a conglomerate of beliefs and traditions so diverse that it was possible to find groups of Hindus whose beliefs had nothing in common. In fact, sometimes it was impossible to find *any* beliefs in common among the groups. Still, Dirk and Angelika studied *Brahman*—the greater Self or God—as well as Truth-Consciousness-Bliss. Disappointed, Dirk and Angelika finally admitted that they found no absolute truth in Hinduism.

Nor did they find it in witchcraft or paganism. Yet the pursuit of truth was a journey that they both enjoyed. The only thing that marred their happiness was the persistent tracts that someone kept slipping under their door.

After three years, Dirk rubbed a weary hand over his eyes and admitted one absolute truth to Angelika. "There aren't enough people in the village interested in witchcraft to keep the bookstore in business."

With great sorrow, they closed its doors.

WHEN GOD COMES TO CALL

Down but not out, Dirk and Angelika rode the buoyant wave of optimism that comes from youth into yet another new venture. They both went to school to become hairdressers. Renting a home with a separate entrance they could use for a salon, they opened their doors for business. They enjoyed working together and being at home with Lorne after school.

Mornings were the busiest time of their day, but one odd weekday in November of 1999, Angelika had a cancellation and found herself with a midmorning break. Walking through the house, she did something she'd never done on a workday. Sinking into a chair, she turned on the television and saw a man talking about spiritual things. She was about to change the channel, when something gave her pause.

This guy is very spiritual if you ignore what he says about Jesus and the Bible, she thought. The following morning, both Angelika and Dirk's clients cancelled at the same time. "Dirk, come listen to this man on television," Angelika said. Settling onto the sofa, they turned on the television and listened to the man preach from the Bible.

"That beats all I ever heard," Dirk said.

Back to their busy schedules, Dirk and Angelika taped the program each morning and watched it each evening. Each new revelation was more amazing than the last. At the end of each broadcast, the viewing audience was offered a chance to pray the prayer of salvation.

One evening, Angelika had an epiphany. *Jesus is the absolute truth that I've searched for my whole life!* As the program wound down, she turned to Dirk and, eyes sparkling, asked, "Do you want to pray the prayer?"

"Let's go for the whole thing!" he agreed.

Together they bowed their heads and asked God to forgive their sins. They asked Jesus to be their Savior and the Lord of their lives. At that moment, a miracle greater than divine healing occurred, a miracle greater than raising the dead. In the twinkling of an eye, Dirk and Angelika Van Battum's spirits were resurrected. In one swoop of divine grace, they became new creatures in Christ Jesus. God bestowed upon them all the rights and privileges Jesus won on Calvary.

They wrote to the television ministry to share their decision, and a few weeks later they received a book in the mail. In it, Angelika found another example of the prayer of salvation. "I want to make sure we prayed correctly," she told Dirk and Lorne. "I'm going to read the prayer, and you repeat it after me." The three of them prayed the prayer of salvation as written in the book.

"Now I think we've got it right," Angelika said with a sigh of relief.

Convicted by the Holy Spirit, Dirk and Angelika looked around their home with new eyes. It was filled with tarot cards, books on witchcraft, and symbols of the occult worth hundreds of dollars.

"We've got to get rid of this stuff," Dirk said.

"We can't give it away or sell it," Angelika agreed. "We've got to destroy it."

Nine-year-old Lorne helped them clean house, speaking to the spirits attached to the artifacts. "Get out of here!" he commanded, tossing tarot cards into boxes to be destroyed. "I don't want you around me!"

With the house cleared of the counterfeit, Dirk and Angelika realized that they had nothing that reflected God. "We need a Bible," Dirk said. "Wait! I've got one my mother gave me years ago!"

Dirk dusted off the Bible and the family gathered to read it. Stumbling over the King James wording, they gave up in defeat.

Not long afterwards, Dirk announced, "I think we should find a church."

"That's going a little too far," Angelika hedged.

"The man on television *said* we needed a church family," Dirk insisted.

"I wonder how we're supposed to find one."

Dirk picked up the newspaper and turned to the religious section. Reading the list of churches in the area, he pointed to the last one. "Here it is, the Victory Church of Penticton."

The following Sunday, Dirk, Angelika, and Lorne joined the church. With Christmas only a month away, they bought one another their heart's desire—new Bibles in simple English.

The Greatest Gift

The lights on the Christmas tree twinkled red, blue, and green, casting a warm glow over the packages wrapped in happy colors. Dirk and Angelika circled the tree like children, feeling the weightiness of the gifts. Angelika counted the days until Christmas, dreaming of owning her own Bible. Not since her first doll had she wanted anything so much.

On Christmas Eve, Angelika lay wrapped in warm blankets and remembered the way she'd cried herself to sleep as a child. *Tomorrow I'm getting absolute truth for Christmas!* Shivering with delight, she was too excited to sleep.

The next morning, Dirk and Angelika opened their new Bibles with reverence. Angelika loved the smell of leather and the sound of each page crinkling as she turned it. "Listen to this!" she said, reading a passage.

"Where did you find that?" Dirk asked with excitement. They read their Bibles for hours that day and well into the night. They pored over the truth bound between the covers during every free moment for weeks.

One Sunday a few months later, a man introduced himself after church. "You're new here aren't you?" he asked.

"We're new to the church, but we've lived in Naramata for several years," Dirk replied.

"Really? What do you do there?"

"We own a hair salon now, but before that we owned a bookstore."

"I know!" the man said, his eyes lit with a warm smile. "You owned Aradia Bookstore! I used to slip gospel tracts under your door."

"You?" Dirk and Angelika asked with a collective gasp.

"That's not all," the man answered with a laugh. "A whole group of us from this church used to do prayer walks around your block praying for your salvation."

It all made sense: the coincidence of two mornings with no business, happening to turn on the television, how they'd been drawn to the gospel in a way they'd never been before, how they'd taped the broadcast and prayed the prayer of salvation. God had even led them to clean everything having to do with witchcraft out of their home. And it was God who led them to this very church.

"God is so good," Angelika whispered, choked by her tears. "Thank you for your prayers."

MOST OF ALL, THEY ARE GRATEFUL FOR THE GREATEST GIFT OF ALL—JESUS. HE GAVE THE WORLD ABSOLUTE TRUTH.

Angelika, Dirk, and Lorne Van Battum are forever grateful for the prayers of those who cried out to God for their salvation. But most of all, they are grateful for the greatest gift of all...*Jesus.*

He gave the world absolute truth for Christmas.

FINDING A FAMILY

Phillip Goudeaux elbowed his way past the people talking in hushed tones and stood over his father's bed. Looking down at the drawn, life-drained face that had frowned upon him for almost twenty years now, his voice was choked with emotion. "Dad?"

His father opened his eyes and looked at Phillip with the familiar loveless stare. Then he turned away.

Phillip felt a seam in his soul rip apart. *Dad, don't do this to me. Don't leave me like this.* Blinking back tears, Phillip tried again. "Dad, I want to talk to you."

Shoulders stiff and jaw set, the man shifted away from his son.

"Dad…"

He refuses to acknowledge my presence!

The moment in all its agony summed up Phillip's life. He'd never fit in. He'd never been good enough to win his father's love. Rejection wasn't a new experience for the lanky, teenage boy; it just didn't get easier with time.

As Phillip grew up in the poorest section of Sacramento, the other black kids had taunted him early on because his caramel skin was a shade lighter than theirs. "Hey, white boy!" "Redneck!" "Honkey!"

At school the white kids hissed, "Tar Baby!"

Phillip had grown up where prostitutes and drug dealers ruled the streets. He'd watched wide-eyed as drug deals went wrong. He'd witnessed every kind of bloodbath—beatings…stabbings…shootings. He'd seen it all, and the gruesome scenes haunted him at night when the lights were out. Life in his neighborhood had been one long, hard lesson in self-defense. Once he got big enough to fight, those who insulted him learned never to do it again.

But now, confronted with his father's frail form, he knew he was whipped. This was a battle he would never win. Eyes stinging and heart breaking, he stumbled from the room. An old woman stopped him. A hand on his arm and deep wisdom in her soul, she whispered. "Son, he *ain't* your daddy."

Phillip flinched in spite of himself. *This old woman is nuts,* he thought. *Everyone knows he's my dad.* She wouldn't give up. Following him outside she said, "Not only is *he* not your daddy, that woman over there is your mother."

Phillip's world tilted off center. *I know my own mother! I've known her all my life!*

The old woman hurried off as the young woman she'd pointed out walked up. "Do you want to take a ride?" she said, less of a question than a statement. Phillip followed her to her car and rode with her through the neighborhood streets. Silent, his fists clenched, he stayed ready to respond to the crushing blow life was about to deliver.

The woman parked in front of an electronics shop, and Phillip followed her onto the sidewalk. "I'm your mother," she said, her words slugging him like an invisible attacker. "That man," pointing to a man in the store window, "is your father.

"I didn't know I was pregnant when he left to go to war some twenty years ago," she explained. "I was young and scared, and I didn't know what to do. When you were three months old, I gave you to Tanyia, the only mother you've ever known."

Phillip's reaction was double-edged. He shook with rage as he realized his whole life had been a web of lies and deceit. But as his anger simmered, he couldn't suppress a bubble of hope rising from within. *At least now I can meet my real family*, he reasoned. *Maybe at last I'll fit in.*

Phillip met his mother's family first. A French Creole, she'd married a Caucasian man. Their children were blue-eyed blondes. A stunned Phillip started at his siblings' fair skin. They looked at him as if to say, "You're just a n— who wants to ruin our lives!"

Phillip's birth father, of Portuguese and African-American descent, had married a black woman. *Surely they'll accept me,* Phillip reasoned.

"You're just after our father's money!" they accused.

He didn't fit in anywhere. The bitterness that took root in his heart grew into white-hot hatred.

THE MENACING GROWTH OF HATRED

On campus at California State University in the early 70s, the lines of racial demarcation were clear. In the cafeteria, the African-American students sat together at their tables. The white students sat at theirs. The Hispanics stayed in their section, as did the Asians.

Phillip, however, didn't sit with any of them. He'd joined another group altogether—a group that sat wherever they wanted; a group so fearsome that when they staked out their territory nobody of any color dared to trespass on it. If they did, it only happened once.

Phillip had joined the Black Panthers.

As a Black Panther, Phillip was surrounded by others as tormented and angry as he. In their midst, he found the sense of belonging that he'd missed. He felt accepted; a sublime change from a life of continual rejection. The Black Panthers had started out doing good things, like sponsoring feeding programs, but over time the group grew so disgusted with the police that they called them "Pigs." Their disgust flourished in a hot house of anger and burgeoned into a venomous vine of hatred that twisted itself around not only the police, but all white people. Even then it didn't stop. It grew until the Black Panthers hated anyone—black or white—who didn't think the way they thought.

Communistic and atheistic, they sold Mao Tse-tung's little red book, *The Thoughts of Chairman Mao.* Believing that the black man was being deceived by the white man's religion, the group rejected the gospel and took delight in breaking up church services.

At CSU, Phillip's Black Panther status guaranteed him the respect he'd always wanted. Named Minister of Defense by the group, he struck fear in many hearts. All Phillip had to do was step into the hall and the moving mass of students rushing to their next class parted like the Red Sea. One look…one furrowed brow…was enough to cause the most courageous to quake.

He'd earned his reputation through violence.

Nobody messed with the Black Panthers; nobody messed with Phillip. He taught martial arts, marksmanship, and boxing to new recruits. In time, he started so many fights that the university put him on probation.

"Start one more fight," he was told, "and we'll kick you out."

That's simple, Phillip reasoned, *I just won't throw the first punch.*

A wary hush fell over the room when Phillip stepped into the cafeteria. Carrying his meal to the Black Panthers' table, he sat down and took a bite of food. A nervous murmur flittered across the cafeteria before the room hummed again with conversation.

Phillip looked up when someone slid into the seat next to him. A white guy with a goofy grin looked back at him. A collective gasp sucked most of the oxygen out of the room, and all conversation stopped. *Does the guy have a death wish or is he just stupid?* Phillip wondered. The room went still as everyone watched to see what he would do.

I can't throw the first punch, Phillip remembered. *But that shouldn't be a problem, I'll just provoke him.* Assuming his most intimidating stance, Phillip screamed insults at his smiling fellow diner.

He sat there with a stupid grin on his face.

Phillip leaned nose to nose with the guy and insulted his mother.

He just smiled.

Phillip insulted his grandmother.

Nothing bothered him.

Phillip looked at his briefcase. A sticker read, "Rejoice in Jesus!"

"Jesus Freak!" Phillip screamed. *"Holy Roller!"*

It worked. The guy leapt to his feet shouting, "If you mean do I love the Lord, yeah, I sure do!"

Forget probation. I'm gonna hurt him now. Phillip doubled his fist and reared back to strike.

But he couldn't; his arm froze in place.

Putting all his power behind the punch, Phillip tried to knock the smile off that annoying pasty face—forever. But he couldn't move. *What's happening?*

THE GREAT ESCAPE

It started as a snicker, then escalated until everyone in the cafeteria roared with laughter. Phillip Goudeaux, Minister of Defense for the Black Panthers, had been humiliated in front of the whole student body. Unable to throw a punch, he did the only thing he could do.

He ran.

If that weren't bad enough, the white guy chased him, shouting, "Hey, wait! I want to talk to you!"

Phillip outran him. Devastated by the incident, he was too embarrassed to show his face on campus for a couple of days. But the time came when he had to return to classes or drop out. Arriving early to get a donut and hot chocolate before class, Phillip tried to act invisible. Then he heard a familiar voice shout, *"Praise the Lord!"*

It was *him.* Phillip sprinted to class, making a clean escape. For the next three months, Phillip's single goal was to avoid the maniacal white geek who had wrecked his reputation. On a campus of 18,000 students, that shouldn't have been too difficult. However, no matter where he went, the goofy grin was not far behind.

Stepping out of anthropology class into the crowded hallway, Phillip heard words that sent chills rippling down his spine. *"Praise the Lord, Phillip!"*

Dashing into the men's room, Phillip Goudeaux, enforcer for the Black Panthers, hid inside a stall. *What's happened to me? Everywhere I go, people laugh at me. I can't sleep at night. This man has ruined my life.*

THE CIRCLE OF LIFE

After three months of Phillip hiding, the guy found him in the library and made so much noise that the librarian kicked them both out.

"What do you *want* with me?" Phillip asked with a sigh of resignation.

"My name's Thomas. If I could just share this little book with you, I'll leave you alone."

"Man, if I'd known that's all you wanted I would have let you do it three months ago."

Phillip watched him pull out a booklet, *The Four Spiritual Laws.* Inside were two circles. One showed Jesus inside the circle. The other showed Jesus outside the circle.

"Each circle represents a life in relationship with Jesus Christ," Thomas explained. "Which one would you say represents your life?"

"Which one do you *want* it to be?" Phillip answered with weariness in every word.

"The one with Jesus in the center," Thomas explained.

"Well, then, that's me. Only one thing, though...I don't believe in God."

"Never mind that," Thomas said. "Just pray this way: God, I don't believe You are real. But *if* You are, come into my life and I'll confess Jesus as my Savior, and make Him Lord of my life."

Anxious to end the encounter, Phillip repeated the words of the prayer. Afterward, Thomas honored his promise and left him alone.

Phillip's life should have been back on track. Thomas didn't dog his steps. Phillip didn't have to hide in the men's room. He didn't have to look over his shoulder every moment of every day. But Phillip Goudeaux was miserable.

I feel like I swallowed a softball, Phillip thought as he tossed and turned, unable to sleep. He hadn't been this miserable even when he was ridiculed as a child. Whatever was wrong with him was worse than when his family rejected him.

It was worse than being humiliated in the cafeteria.

Something in his life went wrong when he prayed that prayer with Thomas. It was as though some unseen force grabbed him and wouldn't turn loose. *It must be God!*

Turning the tables on Thomas, Phillip went in search of him.

Cornering him, Phillip said, "Thomas, I want to receive Jesus into my life."

"Praise the Lord, Phillip!" Thomas said. "First of all, you need to pray and confess that Jesus is the Son of God. Repent of your sins and ask Jesus to sit on the throne of your heart."

Phillip prayed as Thomas directed. Over the next few weeks the strangest thing happened. All the hate, bitterness, and anger dissolved into peace and joy. The pain caused by years of rejection was washed away in the pure love of God.

He was a new man—no question about it—a new man who, once again, just didn't fit in.

"We don't want you in the Black Panthers anymore," Phillip was told. His conversion to Christianity cost him the camaraderie of the group, but it didn't matter.

He went to Tanyia, the mother who'd raised him. "You seem *too* saved," she said.

When Phillip started dating Brenda, a Christian, her pastor didn't think Phillip was quite saved *enough*.

WHEN GOD COMES TO CALL

A DANGEROUS MAN

Refusing to be sidetracked by rejection and resentment, Phillip forged ahead with his college studies. After graduating with a degree in criminal justice in 1974, he went to work for the Southern Pacific Railroad. Phillip had no way of knowing that the Brotherhood of Locomotive Engineers Union had written a clause prohibiting a black man from ever taking the job. When he was promoted to engineer, he found himself embroiled in the battle of his life.

Only this time he refused to fight. "I'm a Christian," he explained.

"The last Christian who worked here got his Bible flushed down the toilet before we threw him off the train," he was told.

Phillip Goudeaux might have been a new creature in Christ, but *nobody* was going to flush his Bible. He explained in specific terms what would happen to any man who tried. After a long pause, each of the men walked away.

Phillip, the new engineer, posted notices announcing the newly formed Railroad Christian Fellowship. Over the next eight years, more than three hundred members joined the Railroad Christian Fellowship, and it went nationwide. Eventually every man who tried to run Phillip off the job was born again, and many of them became strong followers of Christ.

Today, Dr. Phillip Goudeaux pastors Calvary Christian Center in Sacramento, California—one of the most racially mixed churches in America. A dangerous man to the kingdom of darkness, he has led over 100,000 people to the Lord Jesus.

At one time he was the Minister of Defense for the Black Panthers.

Today, he is a minister of the gospel for the kingdom of God. No longer rejected, he is part of God's royal family, a son of the King and joint heir with Christ.

Jesus filled the deepest yearning of his soul.

In Christ, Phillip Goudeaux belongs, and will belong for all eternity.

NOW HE IS PART OF GOD'S ROYAL FAMILY, A SON OF THE KING AND JOINT HEIR WITH CHRIST.

Y ou're fat, you're ugly, and nobody will ever love you," LuLu Roman's grandmother hissed as she tugged the child's teal corduroy jumper over her head. At three years old, LuLu had heard those words so often that they echoed in her mind night and day. Following her grandmother to the car, she tried to shrink…willing herself to be small and lovable.

Too short to see where they were going, LuLu studied the blue vinyl and the silver door handle as they rocked along the road. She craned her neck to catch a glimpse outside when they rolled to a stop.

"Don't dawdle," her grandmother sniped as she flung open the passenger door. LuLu slid out of the car and peered, mystified, at the austere building awaiting them. Her tiny hand jerked upward as her grandmother grabbed it and pulled her along.

Once inside, LuLu sat in a chair in an upstairs hall, swinging her plump legs and looking out the window at children playing.

"Louise, come with me," a strange woman ordered.

"I'm waiting for my grandmother," LuLu explained.

"Your grandmother is gone."

When will she come back to get me? LuLu wondered as she followed the sound of snapping heels down the hallway.

Afraid to ask the question, she waited for the answer to unfold.

That night, LuLu squeezed her eyes shut and tried to sleep in a dormitory bed flanked by other motherless children who lay silent in the twilight. A single, hot tear trembled at the corner of her eyelid, then made the leap and tumbled across her temple into her tangled hair. *Maybe she will come back for me tomorrow.*

The next morning LuLu awoke to the sound of a shrill whistle. All the children jumped out of bed and hurried to obey. Terror-filled days and sleepless nights passed as LuLu realized that she wouldn't be going home again.

A medical examination required on admission to the orphanage revealed that LuLu had a serious thyroid problem. Treatment was administered promptly. It did not, however, make her the petite, adorable child she dreamed of being.

"Fatty, fatty two-by-four; can't get through the kitchen door!" The children's mocking ridicule was relentless. Almost a thousand children in the orphanage confirmed daily that what LuLu had heard all her young life, "*You're fat, you're ugly, and you're unlovable.*"

Getting by with a Little Help

On occasion, LuLu's grandmother did march again up the orphanage sidewalk and take her home to visit her great-grandmother, whose kind smile reminded LuLu of what it felt like to have a home and family. But each visit was marred by stinging barbs that hurt her as deeply as the singsong chants from the other children.

LuLu might never have known untarnished joy if her first grade class hadn't put on a performance of *Hansel and Gretel,* and chosen LuLu—the fat kid—to play the witch. That small token of attention was so delicious that she felt as though her life was over when the last curtain fell.

Watching cars pass in front of the orphanage, LuLu wondered what it would be like to have a mommy...a daddy...brothers...sisters...a room of her own. She would never know. She was certain of that because there were only two ways to obtain them. Your family could come back and take you home, or you could be adopted into a new family.

Nobody wants to adopt a fat kid, LuLu realized as she watched other kids pack their things and leave with new families. She hid from the pain by weeping alone in the closet. But even there in the dark, muffling her sobs by cradling her face in her hands, she couldn't escape it.

Only when LuLu was old enough to attend public high school did she find the relief she'd sought for so long. There, out from under of the shadow of the orphanage, she stepped into a sunny new world of opportunities. Not only did she sing in the operettas, she took roles in school plays and excelled in speech and drama. But the best part of public high school was the drugs. She lived for the Black Mollies that sped her up like a race car at the Indy 500. Flying high, she didn't feel the pain of rejection. She learned to use her quick wit and humor to deflect the cruel remarks.

Back at the orphanage, it seemed that LuLu's every free minute was spent in mandatory church services. Feeling like the Bible was stuffed down her throat, LuLu simmered inside. *God threw me away, and He threw away all these other kids too.* As soon as she turned eighteen and graduated from high school, LuLu decided to leave the orphanage—and the church—forever. *That's enough of that!* she thought, wiping her hands of God.

WHEN GOD COMES TO CALL

Out on her own, LuLu got a job at the phone company, but finally free from the strict confines of the orphanage, she released pent-up anger through bad language. When she lost that job, LuLu went with her roommate to amateur night at a nightclub. Standing in the back of the room, she shook her head at the local talent.

"I could do better than that!" LuLu said aloud.

"I'll bet you fifty dollars you can't," a voice said from behind her. LuLu turned and saw an older man. *Fifty dollars!*

"I *can*," she assured him.

"You've got one week to prove it," he said.

Onstage the next week, LuLu had the crowd laughing at her new persona—Dallas, Texas's, Biggest Go-Go Dancer. Her mocking good humor won her a job. Life looked brighter, but drugs cast an ever-darkening pall. They were like the mafia in her life—always demanding more, there was never enough. By now, she mainlined her speed. Veins bruised and battered, she injected herself in the back of her hands, her legs, and even in her jugular. In addition to the speed, she took as many as twenty-five hits of LSD at a time.

Although her humor made people laugh, she was a miserable, unhappy person. She carried a tire chain in her car, and if anyone crossed her, she could swing it with lethal precision.

During the years she worked in nightclubs, LuLu met Buck Owens. "You're the funniest thing I've ever seen!" Buck said. "LuLu, one of these days you're gonna be a big star, and I'll have something to do with it."

"Keep talking, cowboy!" LuLu urged.

WHEN GOD COMES TO CALL

A few years later, a couple of Canadian comedy writers Buck knew came up with a wacky idea for a new television program called *Hee Haw*. They made a list of the talent they would need to pull it off: one gorgeous blonde; one gorgeous brunette; one girl-next-door type; one boy-next-door type; one fat, dumb man; and one fat, dumb woman.

"I've got your girl!" Buck said. "She lives in Dallas!"

At Buck's urging, LuLu boarded a plane for Hollywood. When she arrived at CBS, the first person she met was Carol Burnett. "Shut your mouth, child. You're fixin' to be one of us," Carol said.

Flying high on drugs, LuLu made funny faces while doling her own brand of humor. "My goodness, you're good!" she was told.

"My goodness, give me your money and see how much better I get!" LuLu retorted.

At age twenty-one, LuLu was hired as a regular on *Hee Haw*. With Kornfield Kounty as a backdrop, the show was produced by Yongestreet Productions and filmed in Nashville. Walking down the halls at Channel 5 and Opryland USA, LuLu, whose favorite style of music was acid rock, wondered how she'd gotten there. Even at her young age and drugged state, she realized she was growing up among legends: Minnie Pearl, Roy Clark, Roy Acuff, Buck Owens, Archie Campbell, and Grandpa Jones.

LuLu was a great success on the show; the only time she failed was when she was asked to sing. The tape was never aired. At age twenty-six, it was not her lackluster crooning but her out-of-control drug use that cost LuLu her job at *Hee Haw*. She was arrested for possession of a dangerous substance and watched her life and her career spiral down the drain. Addicted to heavy doses of drugs, she saw no way out. Just when she thought things couldn't get any worse, LuLu discovered that she was pregnant.

I'm an out-of-work junkie and a single mom! Unable to find a way off the drug roller coaster of highs and lows, she took drugs every day of her pregnancy. On November 15, 1972, her son, Damon, was born addicted to drugs and with acute respiratory syndrome.

"There's no way he can survive," the doctor said.

I've killed my kid! she thought. Standing outside the neonatal intensive care, watching her son fight to breathe, LuLu turned to the God she'd rejected. In her own, irreverent way, she prayed. "Yo…Dude! If You're real, I'll make a deal. Let me have my kid, and I'll do whatever You want."

NEW LIFE

Nothing happened, which is just what she expected. Discharged from the hospital, LuLu went back every day to keep vigil over her dying son. Two weeks later, she got a frantic call from one of the doctors.

"You need to get here!" he demanded.

Heart hammering in her ears, LuLu was certain that this was the call she'd been dreading. She pulled up in front of the hospital and saw the doctor pacing outside. "I don't know what to say," he began.

"You better say something!" demanded LuLu, whose tire chain was within easy reach.

"I know you've been told that your son wasn't going to make it," he said. "I'm sorry, but I can't find anything wrong with him."

"What?"

"I wanted you to come here today because I'm going to discharge him."

"You're going to discharge him?" a stunned LuLu asked. "When?"

"Now," said the doctor.

A short while later, LuLu walked back outside with an infant in her arms.

What now? she wondered. In what seemed to LuLu to be another miracle, Sam Lovullo, producer of *Hee Haw*, stepped in like a hero and saved the day. Generous and kind, he became the father that LuLu had never known. He made sure that LuLu and Damon would survive.

Six months later, LuLu was busted a second time for drug possession. Facing serious prison time, for three days she lay in her jail cell in an agony of drug withdrawal. Desperate for a fix, as soon as she was released on bail, she hit the street in search of drugs.

"Louise?" LuLu turned at the sound of her name and saw Diane, a friend from the orphanage. Needing a fix too bad to linger, she gave Diane her phone number and hurried on.

Diane and her roommate, Paula, called and started showing up on a regular basis at LuLu's house. They brought groceries, baby food, and cleaning supplies. Suspicious, LuLu demanded the truth. "What do you want?"

"I want to take you to my church," Diane explained.

"You know better than that!" LuLu snapped.

"LuLu, listen, I've really found Jesus! Just go with me. *Please?"*

It was guilt over Diane and Paula's kindnesses that drove LuLu to wear long sleeves to cover her track marks and walk into Beverly Hills Baptist Church in Dallas, Texas. The first thing she noticed was the joy; there wasn't a sad face in the crowd—except her own.

The pastor, Howard Conatser, walked down the aisle and took LuLu's hands in his own. "I know who you are," he said, "and I want to introduce you to my church." After the service, people flocked to LuLu...*touching her!* At twenty-six, LuLu had never heard the words, "I love you." She had never been held as a child, and being touched made her anxious.

JOY COMES IN THE MORNING

Over the next few weeks, Diane, Pastor Conatser, and the church rallied around LuLu with an outpouring of love. Shocked by the experience, LuLu found herself in the pastor's office with Diane, discussing her life and her addiction.

"You don't have to be this way," the pastor explained. "You can give it all to Jesus." Grabbing at the shred of hope, LuLu prayed and asked Jesus to be the Lord of her life. No sooner had she finished praying than she felt as though a two-thousand-pound yoke had been lifted from her shoulders.

The next morning, LuLu got up and started cleaning house. At noon, she looked at the clock and froze in panic. Calling Diane, she said, "You'd better get over here and sit with me. I just realized I haven't had any drugs since yesterday so I'm about to go into withdrawal. I apologize in advance for whatever I'll say to you."

Diane rushed to LuLu's side and they sat down to wait for the symptoms of withdrawal. They never came.

Overwhelmed by God's love, LuLu told her pastor, "I want to sing to Jesus!"

"Great!" he said. "You can sing Sunday morning."

LuLu sang, and this time her performance wasn't on a tape that could be kept off the air. It was live. When LuLu was out of town, the pastor swore the congregation to secrecy. Nobody was to tell her that her singing was awful. "Let her sing," the wise pastor instructed.

Week after week and month after month, LuLu sang of her love for Jesus. As time passed, the most extraordinary thing happened. God met her faithful love with His gift. When that happened, not only did LuLu's singing become beautiful, but the power of God wrapped itself around each note and ministered to those who heard her.

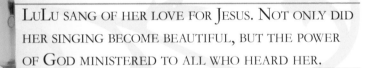

LuLu sang of her love for Jesus. Not only did her singing become beautiful, but the power of God ministered to all who heard her.

GOD RESTORES

Less than a year later, LuLu was asked to fly to Hollywood to give her testimony on Kathryn Kuhlman's television program. Afterward she stopped by CBS to the offices of the producers of *Hee Haw*.

"May I help you?" someone asked.

"Marcia!" LuLu responded.

"LuLu?" LuLu's countenance had changed so much that her old friends didn't recognize her.

"What's *happened* to you?" they asked.

"I gave my life to Jesus," she explained. Standing there, LuLu threw back her head and sang the words of an old gospel song. *"Blessed assurance, Jesus is mine!"*

When the last note faded, they were all in tears.

"LuLu, will you come back to *Hee Haw?"*

"I'll pray about it," LuLu promised. "But if God lets me come back, I want to sing for Jesus."

For the next twenty-five years, LuLu Roman performed on *Hee Haw*. At her insistence, gospel music was introduced to the show. Today she sings in concerts and has released a new album, *Orphan Girl*.

It wasn't just LuLu's career that blossomed under the Master's touch; her family life bloomed as well. "No one ever taught me how to be a mother," she explained to her two sons, Damon and Justin. "So I'll tell you what I'm going to do. I'm going to love you every day of your life. I'm going to tell you every day how much I love you and how proud I am of you. If you have any questions, ask me and I'll find the answers."

LuLu only knew to do for her sons what Jesus did for her. Every day in hundreds of ways He let her know how much He loved her. He made sure she knew how proud He was of her.

LuLu takes personally the words in Jeremiah 29:11–13: *"For I know the thoughts that I think toward you, says the LORD, thoughts of peace and not of evil, to give you a future and a hope. Then you will call upon Me and go and pray to Me, and I will listen to you. And you will seek Me and find Me, when you search for Me with all your heart."*

Even back when LuLu was abandoned in an orphanage, God had a plan for her life, and she's enjoying every moment of it. It's been thirty-four years since she gave her heart to Jesus and waited for the agony of withdrawals.

The fact that those withdrawals never came is a daily reminder of who she is.

No longer an orphan, she is the daughter of the King.

A Love Song Older Than Time

our-year-old JR Polhemus strangled, choking as he struggled to suck great gasps of air into his screaming lungs. His ribcage strained like a broken accordion, the muscles across his shoulders taut with trying. He craved oxygen like life itself but his airway refused to let it gain entrance.

Not again! *his mother thought, her hands fluttering around JR like a bird beating against a cage in a vain attempt to free him. She breathed hard and fast as though by doing so she could somehow help her son. "The doctor's on his way," she said as she propped him against fluffy white pillows that contrasted with the sallow skin stretched across his cheeks. His lips were blue; his eyes wide chocolate saucers of fear.*

"I've given him the medicine but nothing seems to help," JR's mother said as the doctor rushed into the room.

JR's heart rate shuddered. "Call an ambulance!" the doctor barked.

As the ambulance screamed its way to the hospital, the child gave up his fight to live. "Hurry!" the doctor shouted as he started the resuscitation.

Hours later, JR's parents sat beside his bed, keeping vigil over their son. "JR, you died on the way to the hospital," his mother explained. "Isn't it great that Dr. Hiner brought you back?"

JR's eyes blinked open, his little face earnest and intense. "It wasn't the doctor who brought me back, Mama," he said. "It was Jesus."

JR's parents looked at one another with raised brows. His father, a Yale graduate, was an atheist. Neither of his parents were Christians.

Where had he heard that name?

...The memory seemed like a dream as twenty-three-year-old JR Polhemus strolled through a deserted golf course under a moon that shone like a silver globe against the India-ink sky. His chest—now sturdy and broad from years of athletic training—expanded as he breathed deep swallows of the night air. Oxygen danced through his body to the rhythmic tune of crickets and katydids as he thought of the childhood years he spent sick and weakened by an ongoing battle for breath when his old foe, asthma, sucked the air out of his lungs.

Who would have guessed back then that his love of sports would one day help him push past the weakness brought on by his condition? Who would have imagined he could ever play football and wrestle—much less end up as a coach?

JR stood on a manicured green, tilted his head heavenward, and grimaced at the irony. In the past two years since graduating from college, he'd enjoyed a good life, earning a living doing what he loved. Yet, even so, he felt unsettled... *restless.* Gazing up into a universe spangled with stars that winked and stared back at him, he asked aloud the question that plagued him.

"Is this all there is? Is there nothing more to life?"

His mind played over scenes he'd watched so often growing up—his parents entertaining wealthy friends with cocktail parties and shallow conversations. As if on cue, an unexpected breeze kicked up at the thoughts, then faded as quickly as it came. It reminded him of years gone by when kids at school pursed their lips and blew brief gusts across the tops of empty soda bottles, playing them like instruments. JR knew that if it were possible to hold his heart aloft in the breeze right now, it would moan, deep and low, just like those bottles did. It would sing a hollow song and groan for something more.

There *had* to be a deeper meaning to life. He knew it. But what? He'd gone to a dead church when he was twelve years old and dismissed Christianity as boring. Still, he needed spiritual answers and he would search the whole world if necessary to find them.

Just before JR quit his job and began that search, the first step of his journey took him to the Universalism Church in New York City for an Eastern religions meditation seminar. From there, he moved on to what he considered *real* enlightenment—Zen Buddhism, a spiritual philosophy that appealed to JR because of its athletic discipline and because it was free of judgment. A faithful devotee, he knelt before a statue of Buddha and meditated morning and evening.

The meditation did bring JR a kind of superficial peace. It wasn't very deep, but it anchored him. Letting his hair grow long, he decided that an alternate social experience might help him go deeper, so he moved to California and joined a commune. Life took on a slower pace as he worked the ground to grow food for the commune's co-op. Being part of a wide extended family made him feel included and accepted. The pot he smoked numbed him to the barrenness of his own soul. Taking LSD distracted him from it too, entertaining him with mental fireworks of color and bizarre designs.

Still, the emptiness lingered.

Truth be told, the soft breeze through the redwoods and the animals in the commune helped settle the restlessness in JR along with meditation, marijuana, hashish, and LSD. It wasn't just the cattle he enjoyed either—it was the occasional presence of Cowboy Ralph, a rancher who stopped by now and then to lend JR and his friends a hand. JR felt drawn to Ralph in a way that he didn't experience with most people. He was a living example of the old proverb, "Still waters run deep." That was Ralph. Inside him something was deep and peaceful…and real. Too bad he was a Christian, but even so, for some reason Ralph liked these crazy, animal-raising, commune hippies and enjoyed helping them whenever he could.

That's why, on that one particular afternoon, it was no surprise to JR as he leaned against the fence to hear the sound of tires on gravel. He looked up to see Ralph's pickup raising dust. When the door swung open and Ralph slid from beneath the steering wheel, his shirtsleeves were already rolled up. As always, he was here to work.

He grinned a greeting at JR and his two friends, exchanged hellos, then hoisted a bale of hay to his shoulder and worked alongside them until the chores were done. Nothing unusual about that. He did it all the time.

Just before he left that day, however, Ralph shook up the routine—and JR right along with it. He stopped beside his pickup and looked back at them with a flash in his eye JR hadn't seen before. In response, JR felt the hair rising on his arms like it did just before a lightning storm.

"The three of you are all going to come to know Jesus," Ralph said, his eyes squinting against the sun. "But *you*," he said, nodding at JR, "you'll go through some real dark times first."

Slapping his hat against his jeans, Ralph nodded good-bye and drove away.

Jesus? JR wondered. *What's that about?*

TO THE ENDS OF THE EARTH

In 1971, at age twenty-five, JR decided the commune hadn't supplied all the spiritual answers he needed, so he struck out again on a worldwide search for the meaning of life. Hitchhiking across the United States to Montreal, Canada, he flew to Dublin, Ireland. He played his guitar in Dublin Park and met a family who needed help baling hay. While there, he visited a Catholic monastery.

From there, JR hitchhiked through England, Germany, Switzerland, and Italy. In Scotland, he spent two weeks in a Tibetan monastery. In Greece, he spent a week with a multimillionaire and later lived in a bamboo hut on the island of Mikanos.

From Greece, he traveled to Israel, where he met a Christian couple. They were more intellectual than experiential, so he soon lost interest in them. Drawn to Israel, however, he determined to stay awhile and moved with some newfound friends onto a yacht. He spent his days on the deck, looking out over the sapphire water off the coast of Israel and inhaling marijuana and hashish. Surrounded by beauty and living in leisure, JR found himself smack in the middle of the quintessential good life. But even so, he still felt...*bored*. Empty. Restless.

One of his friends came up with an idea to break the monotony. "Hey, let's rent a kayak and have some fun."

"That's cool," JR agreed, "as long as we can take our stash with us."

"No way! We might get caught with it," another friend argued. "We'll smoke it all and then go out."

Outvoted, JR settled back and enjoyed the drugs. Later, having finished all the drugs on hand, the men took a kayak out into choppy water.

"Don't float out of Israeli waters!" the kayak owner warned. "It's dangerous!"

High on drugs, the two friends laughed as they paddled the kayak away from shore. What would life be like if you didn't flirt with danger, push the limits of the envelope... paddle outside the boundaries of Israeli waters?

The gunboat that chased them down wasn't filled with leggy Dutch girls like those JR and his friends had left behind on the yacht. It was manned by men with machine guns who reflected the political tension in the Middle East. JR and his friend Joe were arrested, blindfolded, and transported to a prison in Amman, Jordan. Sitting in a dank cell, JR sobered up enough to feel deep fear.

"If you'd listened to me and taken the drugs with us on the kayak," JR said to his friend in a whisper, "we'd never see sunlight again."

His friend nodded in agreement, terrified that even without the drug charges they might rot in jail for the rest of their lives.

When JR and his friends were extradited from Jordan to Israel, they were locked up in Cell Block Eight of the Jerusalem prison. It was a hellhole the likes of which JR had never imagined. In filth, darkness, and danger, the men were caught in the constant tension between Arab and Jewish prisoners.

Afraid to sleep, JR stared into the dark as a young boy was raped. The sound of someone screaming echoed off the stone walls. A stunned JR realized the screams were his own, his way of trying to stop the horrible act.

Weeks passed with no prospects of release. Then…finally…a note smuggled out of the prison alerted someone that JR and his friend needed help. Palms were greased at $450 each, and a few weeks later they staggered out of jail and into the crowded streets of Jerusalem. After six months traveling the world, JR was no closer to finding the meaning of life, but his stint in jail made him wary of staying in the Middle East. After waiting two weeks for his passport to be returned, JR flew back to California and returned to the commune he had left months earlier.

Settled again in the routine of commune life, JR assumed he was home free. But in reality, he just traded a natural prison for a spiritual one. He stumbled into it in early 1973 when a woman who wrote books specializing in New Age phenomenon set her sights on him. "I recognize supernatural gifts in you," she explained. "I'm going to train you to channel spirits."

Once a month, JR traveled to San Jose for training. With her guidance, master spirits were channeled through him. His education included séances, and he even learned about Jesus. "Jesus was one of the great masters," she explained.

During one weekend at a New Age center, another woman "enlightened" JR by spiritually opening his third eye. Hungry for the supernatural, JR had no idea that he was slipping deeper and deeper into darkness and death. He didn't realize he'd been locked into a cell of spiritual deception as horrific as Cell Block Eight. He didn't even try to smuggle out a prayer for help.

He didn't know he needed it.

In November of 1973, help came anyway. John and Suzanne Hunter, a couple of JR's friends from his early commune days, stopped by to visit. Suzanne had been there the day Cowboy Ralph gave his strange prophecy. She too had been told that she would one day "come to know Jesus."

What JR didn't know when John and Suzanne walked through the door was that since he'd last seen them, that prophecy had been fulfilled. The couple had given their lives to Christ.

John clapped JR on the back, glad to see him again, and took in the scene around him. The house overflowed with people, drugs, and a Buddhist altar. Demon spirits had free reign of the place. Knowing that nothing could be accomplished until he'd dealt with the demonic, John locked himself in the bathroom and prayed, using his spiritual authority to clean the environment.

Then, for three hours, he and his wife presented the gospel to their old friend. JR listened to every word, but it wasn't their delivery that caught his attention. It wasn't their presentation of the plan of salvation that made him catch his breath. Nor was it their knowledge of the Bible.

It was *them*. Although he'd searched the world, JR had never seen anything like it. John and Suzanne Hunter weren't the same people he once knew. The difference in them was radical and profound.

They hadn't just found an answer to life. They'd discovered *new life itself.*

Their *world* hadn't changed. *They* had changed.

They were exactly what they claimed to be—new creatures. They had that same peace like a deep river that JR had seen in Ralph.

What they had was real.

It was life-shattering.

It was *Jesus.*

The same Jesus who'd brought him back from death at the tender age of four.

> WHAT THEY HAD WAS REAL. IT WAS LIFE-SHATTERING. IT WAS *JESUS.*

The same Jesus who'd warned him through Ralph of the dark danger he would experience in the Middle East.

Their truth was more radical than anything JR had ever imagined. Whatever had transformed them from turbulent rapids into deep wells of peace—*that's* what JR wanted. Bowing his head, he asked Jesus to be his Savior and the Lord of his life.

His conversion experience wasn't dramatic. He didn't see angels or feel goose bumps. But from the depths of his heart he prayed, "Lord Jesus, if You can do anything with my life…it's Yours."

Thrilled beyond belief at the new life within him, JR couldn't wait to tell his New Age teachers about Jesus. They didn't greet the news with enthusiasm. Their anger was rabid.

JR went to work in a nursery next door to a church. There, God's answer to JR's prayer continued to unfold. God began to do something with his life. The transformation began when the pastor of the church befriended JR and invited him to attend a pastor's conference. There, he received a call from God to pastor. JR answered the call by applying for and—miracle of miracles—receiving a full scholarship to Princeton Theological Seminary. During his studies, he met a minister with a powerful healing ministry. A man of great wisdom, he took JR under his wing and, through deliverance, helped catapult him into God's will.

By the time JR graduated from Princeton, his parents and brothers had seen the radical change in him and accepted Christ themselves.

Today, JR Polhemus pastors The Rock in Castle Rock, Colorado. He is married with two grown children and two grandchildren, who all are part of a strong, rapidly growing body of believers. It isn't JR's oratory skills that cause people to flock there. It isn't just his knowledge of the

Bible. What draws people is the man, and the deep rivers of peace that flow from him as a result of the Answer he has found.

If it were possible to hold JR Polhemus's heart in the breeze these days, it would no longer echo with a hollow, mournful sound. It would sing the joyful song of the redeemed—the song that speaks gratefully of Jesus of Nazareth as the answer to all of life's questions. That is the song that wooed JR and caused a longing in him that nothing else could fill.

It's a love song older than time.

*E*xploding *with unbridled energy, young Nikki Nikitin scampered through the communal flat in St. Petersburg, Russia, and leapt onto his grandmother's bed. Brown hair standing on end, he jumped up and down, higher and higher. Mid-leap, he noticed the corner of a book peeking from under his grandmother's pillow and dropped to his knees to take a closer look. His bright eyes burned with curiosity as he scanned the handwritten words.*

"Nikki!" his grandmother hissed, grabbing the book from his hand. Glancing around with furtive caution, she stuffed it under clothes in the bureau drawer. "Never touch that again," she whispered, her lips trembling. "Never tell anyone what you saw."

Little Nikki swallowed his questions. The words in the book must be very dangerous to make his grandmother quake in terror.

Secrets, Nikki thought, walking down the street in St. Petersburg. *Russia is full of them.* Even the art that he loved held secret messages written in a code that Nikki hadn't been able to break.

He lifted his collar against the drizzle and dank, gray air and quickened his pace, eager to see the masterpieces again. Raising his eyes to the skyline, Nikki drank in the timeless beauty of spiral-domed cathedrals and palaces whose magnificent architecture gave proof that Russia had once been one of the richest nations on earth. His journey ended at his favorite place—the Hermitage. Stepping inside, he sighed and relaxed in the presence of old, familiar friends as he lost himself among priceless paintings by Rembrandt, Leonardo da Vinci, and Picasso.

Unlike the canvas-borne beauties that stole Nikki's heart when he began studying them at the tender age of five, Nikki's life was no work of art. He had been born into the stark, utilitarian world of a Siberian prison camp where his mother was in charge of training people to be Communists. Later, after moving to St. Petersburg, she'd studied at the university and become a nuclear scientist. A high-ranking Communist, she barked orders all day. That didn't change when she came home to her son each night.

The only softness Nikki ever knew was in the feathered brushstrokes left behind by the great painters of eras gone by. No wonder he was learning by the age of fourteen to restore their priceless works. They were his only passion. Yet now, at age twenty, Nikki was no longer satisfied by just restoring them. He wanted to know the meaning of the images they portrayed. Somehow, he'd learned, the pictures were connected to God—a very dangerous subject in the Soviet Union.

Believing in God could cost you: at the least, admittance to a mental institution; at the worst, a state-supported stay in a Siberian prison camp. Bibles were forbidden in Russia. Like so many other things here, the thought of them inspired not faith but fear.

Such was everyday life in Russia. Steeped in fear.

More terrifying than God and the Bible were the foreigners who believed in them. Foreigners, the government warned, came to steal Russian technology. All Americans were with the C.I.A. Talking to a foreigner was a serious crime, punishable by imprisonment. Being caught with fifty dollars of foreign currency carried a sentence of eight years.

The fact was, Russians lived in perpetual fear of being caught—for any reason or for no reason at all—by the police. They worried as they watched them pick some random person out of a crowd, follow him, frisk him, and arrest him. Wondering if they would be next, even law-abiding citizens cringed at the sound of footsteps from behind. The whoosh of an elevator opening on your floor at night was terrifying.

There was even distrust among the closest neighbors. When twenty families in a communal flat shared one kitchen and bathroom, on a good day, you were up by four in the morning to get to the bathroom first. Stress built like a pressure cooker when one family bought a chicken and tried to eat it while nineteen families watched with empty bellies. When hungry people got desperate, who knew what they would do?

It was no surprise to Nikki that people didn't smile much in Russia. They were too afraid.

For most of his life, Nikki had been no different. He'd kept a low profile, followed the communist rules, and stayed away from foreigners. Yet not even the specter of police reprisal could stem Nikki's hunger for answers to the forbidden secrets hidden in his beloved art. One picture in particular aroused his curiosity. The artist spent twenty-four years on the painting. What was so important that a man would spend a quarter of a century capturing it?

The scene portrayed John the Baptist with Jesus at the Jordan River. Yearning to know what the story meant, Nikki and his friend Paul hatched a plan to find out.

Candles flickered, casting a golden hue over the Russian Orthodox Church, the only legal church in Russia. The priest, wearing a long, ceremonial beard, robes, and a large gold cross, greeted them.

"How can we know more about God?" Nikki asked.

"Guys," the priest said with a condescending smile, "this is not your business. You just light candles, and we'll take care of the rest."

Nikki stepped out of the dark church and looked around his beloved city. He saw references to God everywhere, but the mystery of how to reach Him remained a well-kept secret. Depressed, he trudged home through the twilight.

A few days later, on November 5, 1986, Nikki and Paul were walking down the street when a tour bus stopped near-by. Before they could make their escape, tourists surrounded them. Terrified that the police might see them, they slipped through the crowd. Even as they fled, Nikki couldn't help but notice the strangest thing about the tourists.

They were all smiling.

Two hours later, Nikki and Paul wandered into St. Isaac's Cathedral, where their friend worked restoring the art. Fear rippled down Nikki's spine when one of the tourists from the bus approached him.

He must be with the C.I.A. and followed us here! Terrified, Nikki was about to bolt when the man pointed at a Bible mosaic on the wall and said the one thing guaranteed to stop him in his tracks.

"I know what those pictures mean. Would you like to know?"

Heart beating like a jackhammer, Nikki looked around. He wanted to know what those mosaics meant, but it was too dangerous to talk here. The stranger agreed to meet them on a bridge across town.

Is this a trap? Nikki wandered when he arrived at the bridge. They waited an hour, but the man never arrived. Dejected, they went on their way.

Later that day, passing by the same bridge, Nikki saw the tourist. *This is our third chance meeting in one day!* Nikki realized. Curiosity overcame his fear, and Nikki and Paul walked over to talk to the forbidden stranger.

Joy radiating from his eyes, the man agreed to tell Nikki and Paul the forbidden secret. It was the secret that had been painted, etched, and carved into cathedrals and museums all over Russia. It was a secret that Satan had spent centuries trying to conceal from the nation.

Leaning close, the stranger spoke three words: "God loves you."

THE MAN TOLD NIKKI AND PAUL THE FORBIDDEN SECRET. "GOD LOVES YOU."

No one had ever told Nikki that they loved him. Unsure that *anybody* loved him, the words poured over Nikki like warm oil. Nothing in his life had prepared him for the powerful love that washed over him when the stranger led him in the sinner's prayer.

The man's name was David Esala. Back home in Appleton, Wisconsin, the Lord had put Russia on his heart. *Just one soul,* the Holy Spirit had urged. *Believe me for just one soul.*

An ecstatic David Esala led both Nikki and Paul to the Lord. Before leaving Russia, he gave them a small, red New Testament. Finally, they had access to the great mystery of God.

In English.

Using a Russian/English dictionary, they began the laborious task of translating each word. It was a long, arduous and dangerous job, but they persisted when many people would have given up. The day they translated John 3:16, Nikki blinked back tears. There it was in black and white. *For God so loved the world...*

Although he'd never seen a Bible before, there was an aching familiarity about the words. He bolted upright in bed one night when the memory that had teased his mind washed over him in full bloom. *My grandmother did the same thing! She had a handwritten copy of the Bible hidden under her pillow!* Too afraid to share it with her grandson, she'd taken the forbidden secret to her grave.

SHARING THE GOOD NEWS

Nikki didn't want to do that. With each amazing revelation from the Bible, Nikki and Paul whispered the secret to their friends. The news was too good to keep quiet. Their friends whispered it to others.

It took Nikki and Paul two years to translate the New Testament, but long before they finished, they had a group of people waiting to hear the next verse. Where could they meet?

"It's dangerous to meet at my mother's apartment," Nikki explained. "As a high-ranking Communist, she's required to report all Christians to the police."

"It would be even more dangerous at my mother's house," Paul said. "Did you forget that my mother is a member of the KGB?"

Risking their lives, Nikki, Paul, and their growing band of new believers met at Nikki's mother's apartment while she worked.

Two years later, the Holy Spirit urged Nikki to tell his mother that he was a Christian. Nikki tried to imagine her response. Would she scream at him? Hit him? Report him? *Probably all of the above,* Nikki thought, rubbing moist palms on his jeans.

"I need to talk to you about something," Nikki said, sitting beside his mother. Looking up at him with expectant eyes, she waited for her son to tell her what was on his mind.

Taking a deep breath, Nikki announced, "Mother, God loves you. Jesus loves you. And He's changed my life."

Nikki steeled himself for her reaction, but his mother did the one thing he never imagined. She wept.

Like Nikki, her life had been devoid of love. Hungry to experience God's love for herself, she prayed the sinner's prayer. From that day on, her relationship with Nikki grew deep and rich. As she allowed God to express His love to her, she began expressing her love for Nikki.

Following her conversion, Paul and Nikki grew even more bold about sharing their faith. "So what if we're thrown into prison or sent to a mental institution?" Nikki asked the underground church of new believers. "Jesus paid the ultimate price for us. Are we willing to pay any price for Him?"

GOD MAKES A WAY

Nikki and Paul decided to go public. They chose the place where crowds gathered daily for culture and enlightenment—the Museum of Atheism. They played a guitar and sang, and a crowd soon gathered and listened while Nikki and Paul revealed the forbidden secret: God not only existed, He loved each one of them so much that He sent His Son Jesus to pay the penalty for their sin. They led the crowd in the sinner's prayer as police sirens screamed on their way to arrest them. Slipping through the throngs of people, Nikki and Paul got away that time. They weren't always so fortunate.

One day when Nikki went to the Museum of Atheism to preach, he met a young man named Mitya. Half of his head was shaved and the other half sported long hair. He wore a jacket with the communist symbol upside-down.

"I look like my generation," Mitya explained. "We're lost. We don't know where to go or what to do." Nikki showed him the way to Jesus.

As the underground church grew, Nikki and Paul cried out to God for help in leading them. In 1990, in an unprecedented move, Russia granted visas to those wishing to pursue religious studies. With help from David Esala, Nikki and Paul traveled to the United States, where they enrolled in Bible college. While they were there, in another unprecedented move, the Soviet Union dissolved. Nikki's mother, nuclear scientist and high-ranking Communist, had the privilege of leading the church out from underground.

Back in Russia a year later, Nikki couldn't take in all the changes. Not only was the country morally bankrupt, it was also financially bankrupt. Five years earlier, a thousand rubles had been worth $1500. Now they were worth a quarter. Pornography and organized crime had sprung up overnight.

Nikki grieved for his country—until he stepped into church. For the first time in his life, it was legal for him to worship God in Russia. A thousand people gathered in the public meeting, praising God with all their hearts. Many were saved, healed, and delivered from years of oppression.

Through God's great grace, and because one man cried out for one soul, Nikki and Paul were licensed, ordained ministers of the gospel of Jesus Christ at the exact moment in history when it became legal to worship Him. In a country torn by change, two young leaders had the answers that they needed. That answer had been painted, etched, and sculpted in thousands of places in Russia.

The forbidden secret was a secret no more.

THE "SECRET" OF GOD HAD BEEN PAINTED, ETCHED, AND SCULPTED ALL OVER RUSSIA.

PART THREE

WILL YOU HOLD OPEN THE DOOR?

BY GINA

Now when they heard this, they were cut to the heart, and said to Peter and the rest of the apostles, "Men and brethren, what shall we do?" Then Peter said to them, "Repent, and let every one of you be baptized in the name of Jesus Christ for the remission of sins; and you shall receive the gift of the Holy Spirit. For the promise is to you and to your children, and to all who are afar off, as many as the Lord our God will call." And with many other words he testified and exhorted them, saying, "Be saved from this perverse generation." Then those who gladly received his word were baptized; and that day about three thousand souls were added to them. —Acts 2:37–41

God can save the lost people you love. The testimonies in this book provide stunning evidence of that fact. Whether they're Black Panthers, bad bikers, drug dealers, or tarot card readers, God has the power to redeem sinners of all kinds. He loves them enough to track them down, tackle them, and pull them to His heart.

God wants us to know that.

He *needs* us to know that.

Why? Because we, as believers, open the door for Him to reach them. When we give up on them, the door slams shut. No wonder, since the day the church began, God's Spirit has been pleading with us to keep loving, praying for, and sharing the gospel with the lost. No wonder He urges us without ceasing to obey the last words Jesus spoke in His earthly ministry:

All authority has been given to Me in heaven and on earth. Go therefore and make disciples of all the nations, baptizing them in the name of the Father and of the Son and of the Holy Spirit, teaching them to observe all things that I have commanded you; and lo, I am with you always, even to the end of the age. (Matthew 28:18–20)

Notice Jesus didn't ask us to make disciples of a few open-hearted, easy-to-reach folks. He told us to go after them all. Even the hard cases. Even the ones who laugh and tell us to leave them alone. Even the ones who openly defy the Lord and claim they'll never give their life to Him. God wants us to grip those people with our faith like a lifeguard grips a drowning man and—no matter how they fight us—refuse to let them go.

If we will do that, God can save them. He proved that the first day He launched His fledgling church. He erased any doubt about His saving power by building His first congregation out of the crustiest characters imaginable—the haughty-eyed crowd that gathered in Jerusalem to celebrate the first Pentecost after Jesus' death.

If God could save those folks, He can save anyone. They weren't naïve, untaught people who'd never heard the gospel. They comprised what evangelists sometimes call "a burnt-out harvest field." They had heard the gospel proclaimed by the lips of Jesus Himself. They had seen His signs, they had witnessed His wonders, and they had rejected Him for three solid years.

Their rejection wasn't the quiet, genteel kind, either. They didn't just smile and say, "You know, I'm really not that into this whole Jesus thing right now. But thanks for sharing."

They were rabid in their rejection. The morning of the crucifixion, they joined the rabble on Pilate's patio and, unmoved by his declaration of Jesus' innocence, cried with murderous fury, "Crucify Him!"

That's what I call a tough crowd.

You'd think God would give up on people like that. You'd think He'd choose some fresh-faced, unevangelized group to preach to on that bright Pentecostal morning. But He didn't. He sent Peter to speak to the same calloused, mean-spirited bunch and say:

> *Men of Israel, hear these words: Jesus of Nazareth, a Man attested by God to you by miracles, wonders, and signs which God did through Him in your midst, as you yourselves also know; Him, being delivered by the determined purpose and foreknowledge of God, you have taken by lawless hands, have crucified, and put to death; whom God raised up, having loosed the pains of death, because it was not possible that He should be held by it.* (Acts 2:22–24)

Not exactly a Dale Carnegie speech, was it? Peter's sermon didn't seem likely win friends and influence people. It seemed more likely to inspire the kind of violence Peter so feared a few weeks earlier that he denied even knowing the Lord. Did he consider that possibility as he stomped on the crowd's spiritual toes? Did it occur to Peter that since this group had rejected the Master Himself, logic would dictate they'd also reject His apprentice and shout, "Crucify him too!"

I would think so. Peter had a history of considering such possibilities and responding with the appropriate cowardice. But this time it wasn't just Peter on the witness stand for Jesus. It was Peter filled with and empowered by the Holy Spirit. It was Peter preaching the supernatural gospel of the resurrected Lord Jesus Christ.

That gospel always defies logic. It accomplishes what our human minds deem impossible. It can cut even the most sinister sinners to the heart and leave them crying, *"Men and brethren, what shall we do?"* (Acts 2:37).

As contemporary Christians, we sometimes lose sight of that fact. We let our confidence in the power of the gospel begin to slip. Although we don't mean to, we can wind up treating it like an aging athlete who once performed great feats but can't be expected to do so anymore. Meandering through the book of Acts like sports fans browsing through a hall of fame, admiring yellowed baseball jerseys and crinkled catchers' mitts, we gaze at what the gospel message accomplished in days of old—the three thousand won at Pentecost and the thousands more saved at the Gate Beautiful, the city full of Samaritans who turned to Jesus when Philip preached to them, and the house full of Gentiles who threw Peter's evangelistic team into a panic when they all jumped up and got saved without even waiting for the altar call. "My, my, those were the days, weren't they?" we sigh. "Those were the days."

God never intended it to be so.

He never meant for us to view the soul-saving power of the gospel as a thing of the past. It's the devil who has tried to cultivate that attitude in us. He has clothed himself as an angel of light (see 2 Corinthians 11:14) and spoken to us in compassionate, soothing tones, telling us that the gospel no longer packs the punch it did when Peter preached it.

"That stuff about people being sinners separated from God turns folks off these days," he says. "Nobody wants to hear about Jesus being crucified for the sins of the world anymore. Nobody cares about His death and resurrection. That's old news. People today want a message more culturally relevant than that."

THE ANOINTING FOR SALVATION CAN TRANSFORM THE STONIEST HEARTS INTO CLAY SOFT ENOUGH TO BE SHAPED BY THE POTTER'S HAND.

Such insidious suggestions corrode our confidence in the simple message about the life, death, and resurrection of Jesus and the sinner's need for His saving grace. They leave us wondering if it still appeals to the preferences of sinners and, to use a popular marketing term, "addresses their felt needs."

If it doesn't, why bother to share it with them? Why keep offering them a gospel they don't want?

Because infused into that gospel is the anointing for salvation—an anointing so supernatural it can transform the stoniest hearts into clay soft enough to be shaped by the Potter's hand.

That's what happened on the day of Pentecost. The feisty group that Peter preached to had no desire at all for Jesus. They despised both the Man and His message. They'd made that plain by voting to crucify Him. Yet Peter still declared to them the plain, scriptural truth: that they were sinners in need of the Savior they had murdered, the resurrected Lord Jesus Christ.

In marketing terms, the message sounds like a formula for disaster, and it would have been if Peter had been trying to sell hamburgers or soft drinks. But that's not what he was doing. He was reaching out to the greatest God-rejecters of all time with the only message potent enough to win them: the New Testament gospel.

And win them it did…by the thousands.

Granted, that was two thousand years ago, but in all the years since, the gospel hasn't changed. It can still do today what it did that Pentecostal morning on the sun-toasted streets of Jerusalem. It can arrest the most rebellious rascals around and bring them from darkness to light. It can save fathers and mothers, husbands and wives, children and cousins, aunts and uncles. It can bring friends and acquaintances, even enemies and strangers, into the kingdom of God. It can crack even the hardest cases.

But for the gospel to do so, someone must share it with them. Someone must be bold enough to tell them the good news.

It might be you, or I, or another loving believer. But somebody must do it. Somebody must plant the seed of the Word before the tree of eternal life can grow.

As I discovered when I imagined the grocery store clerk hurling the lettuce at me, that isn't always easy. We may have to pray for Peter's boldness to give us the guts to open our mouths. We may have to ask God to give us words to say because telling people they're in need of a Savior can be challenging. It isn't a comfortable topic of conversation.

Even though the gospel is good news, people don't always respond to it as such. When we tell them about it, they rarely treat us like we're Ed McMahon notifying them they've won the Clearinghouse sweepstakes. Sometimes our good news makes them cranky.

Of course, most of us will never face the predicament Peter did. We'll never have to wonder if the people we tell about Jesus will get cranky enough to kill us. As Christians living in a free nation, that's not our greatest fear.

Our greatest fear is that they will laugh.

There, I said it. The embarrassing truth is that we often bite our tongue and withhold the anointed message of salvation from people because we're afraid they'll think it's silly. In our sophisticated age of science and enlightenment, we feel dumb reciting simplistic phrases such as, *"If you confess with your mouth the Lord Jesus and believe in your heart that God has raised Him from the dead, you will be saved"* (Romans 10:9), or *"He who has the Son has life; he who does not have the Son of God does not have life"* (1 John 5:12).

Give me a break. We might as well tell people, "Everything you need to know about spirituality and eternal salvation, you learned in vacation Bible school." What evolution-indoctrinated, Generation Xer is going to buy that?

Sure, those of us who are already born again believe it. We have humbled ourselves and staked our lives on a plan of salvation so simple it can be presented on a felt board to kindergarteners. We are living testimonies to the truth that all you have to do to revolutionize your life is "repent of sin and ask Jesus into your heart."

But therein lies the dilemma. The sheer simplicity of the message makes it sound ridiculous to some people. Even before we open our mouths, we can imagine them mocking us. "One way to God? What kind of narrow-minded ignorance is that?"

If we could, we'd dress up the gospel in more educated garb and make it sound brainy. But unless we alter the message, it remains as uncomplicated as John 3:16: *"For God so loved the world that He gave His only begotten Son, that whoever believes in Him should not perish but have everlasting life."*

How do we get around that?

According to the Bible, we can't.

To some people, the gospel is going to sound silly. (See 1 Corinthians 1:20–21.) If we make it sound complicated and smart, we'll mess it up.

Just knowing that takes a ton of pressure off us. It sets us free to share our faith with childlike innocence. We don't have to worry anymore about thinking up ways to make the good news sound cool and deep and profound. We can follow the example of Paul—one of the most effective soul-winners of the New Testament—who said he didn't even try to present the gospel *"with wisdom of words, lest the cross of Christ should be made of no effect"* (1 Corinthians 1:17).

> *For the message of the cross is foolishness to those who are perishing, but to us who are being saved it is the power of God.*

For it is written: "I will destroy the wisdom of the wise, and bring to nothing the understanding of the prudent." Where is the wise? Where is the scribe? Where is the disputer of this age? Has not God made foolish the wisdom of this world? For since, in the wisdom of God, the world through wisdom did not know God, it pleased God through the foolishness of the message preached to save those who believe.

(verses 18–21)

Knowing this makes us bolder to share the gospel. It keeps us from thinking we've presented it wrong just because someone shrugs it off as stupid. It liberates us to tell with splendid simplicity who Jesus is, what He has done, and how He has set us free. So what if they laugh? The important thing is not their initial response to the gospel anyway. (Remember how angry my friend Joe was at first? And how insulted my sister's Maharaji-worshipping neighbor Barbara was?) What counts is that people hear it. Once they hear it, it will go to work on them.

> ONCE PEOPLE HEAR AND SEE THAT JESUS HAS SET US FREE, IT WILL GO TO WORK ON THEM UNTIL THEY LONG FOR WHAT WE HAVE FOUND.

Laugh now…get saved later. It happens all the time.

Why is that? Because the gospel isn't just religious information. It's not a spiritual philosophy or an intellectual worldview. The gospel is alive. It contains and imparts the miracle-working strength and energy of God Himself. Paul said it this way:

> *I am not ashamed of the gospel of Christ, for it is the power of God to salvation for everyone who believes, for the Jew first and also for the Greek.* (Romans 1:16)

The Greek word translated *"power"* in that verse is the word *dunamis*. *Strong's Concordance* defines it as "strength power, ability...power residing in a thing by virtue of its nature... power for performing miracles." Sometimes in this day of multi-media Christianity, we get the idea that the power of the gospel is in its presentation. We assume it has greater impact when presented with elegant words or portrayed on a giant screen by skilled actors and surround sound. But that's not so. The gospel can deliver the same spiritual wallop shared one-on-one at a corner table in Starbucks as it does when it's heralded by a three-hundred-member choir at a Christmas pageant.

The power of the gospel is not in its presentation. It's in the message itself and the anointing it carries.

Paul understood this so well that when he preached, he didn't even try to give a polished speech. He delivered his message raw and rough. He said:

> *And I, brethren, when I came to you, did not come with excellence of speech or of wisdom declaring to you the testimony*

of God. For I determined not to know anything among you except Jesus Christ and Him crucified. I was with you in weakness, in fear, and in much trembling. And my speech and my preaching were not with persuasive words of human wisdom, but in demonstration of the Spirit and of power, that your faith should not be in the wisdom of men but in the power of God. (1 Corinthians 2:1–5)

Believe it or not, the scriptural message of salvation carries so much power it can save people even when it's preached by ministers with evil motives. I heard about a man some years back, for example, who decided to scam people out of money by masquerading as a minister. After memorizing the sermons of an authentic gospel preacher, he recited them in his meetings word for word while kicking his legs and whirling his arms like a windmill to appear enthusiastic. Sure enough, people in his meetings got born again. Their hearts were touched and their lives were changed. The power of the message he was preaching did its job despite his bad intentions.

Eventually, the charlatan-preacher was arrested and put in prison for financial fraud. You can probably guess what happened. While he was sitting in prison, he started thinking about the messages he had preached and got saved himself.

That's the power of the gospel. No wonder when Paul was sitting in prison writing the Philippians, he chuckled over the fact that his enemies were trying to irritate him by pretending to be preachers. They thought they were doing Paul a disservice, but he was grateful for their help, and said:

> *Some indeed preach Christ even from envy and strife, and some also from good will: the former preach Christ from selfish ambition, not sincerely, supposing to add affliction to my chains; but the latter out of love, knowing that I am appointed for the defense of the gospel. What then? Only that in every way, whether in pretense or in truth, Christ is preached; and in this I rejoice, yes, and will rejoice.*

(Philippians 1:15–18)

THE GOSPEL ITSELF PRODUCES THE RESULT, NOT OUR PRESENTATION OF IT. IT CAN BEAR FRUIT EVEN FROM DISHONEST LIPS.

Those verses are a colossal encouragement to all of us who hesitate to tell the good news because we're afraid we won't do it effectively. They remind us that the gospel itself produces the results, not our perfect presentation of it. God's message of salvation is so full of power that it bore fruit even when it fell from dishonest lips. How much more can it accomplish when we share it with a pure heart?

Even if we convey it with clumsy phrases, the gospel we share will carry the anointing for salvation. It will drop like a tiny seed into a lost heart and, despite its seeming insignificance, that seed can change everything. Jesus left no doubt about that when He said:

> *What is the kingdom of God like? And to what shall I compare it? It is like a mustard seed, which a man took and put in his garden; and it grew and became a large tree, and the birds of the air nested in its branches.*
>
> (Luke 13:18–19)

Never be discouraged by the unimpressive appearance of the simple gospel. Never let the devil convince you that your little testimony doesn't count. Keep spreading the mustard seed message of Jesus' saving blood, because no matter how small and silly those seeds may seem, they have the capacity to grow up and bless not just one life but multitudes of them.

Mac Gober proved just how true that is. His once-wretched life was touched by one dog-eared gospel tract shoved into his hand outside Western Union. Talk about an unimpressive seed! Mac didn't even want that stupid tract. He tried to get rid of it, but he couldn't. In the end, that one flimsy piece of paper became a seed that helped save not only his life, but the lives of all the young men who've gotten a second chance at Canaan Land. It grew up and became a mighty tree of life in the kingdom of God.

"But I don't know how to plant mustard seeds," you might say. "I'm no preacher. I have no idea how to talk to somebody about Jesus."

Sure you do. Just tell them what He has done for you. That's what the former Madman of Gadara did. He was no preacher either, but he set his hometown on fire for Jesus. He was so grateful to be delivered from the legion of demons that had possessed and tormented him that he wanted to go into the ministry. He even begged Jesus to let him travel with Him. But Jesus said no. He told the no-longer-madman:

> *"Return to your own house, and tell what great things God has done for you." And he went his way and proclaimed throughout the whole city what great things Jesus had done for him.* (Luke 8:39)

Imagine it! Without going to Bible college or even taking one course in evangelism, that man went home and stirred up a citywide revival by becoming a motormouth for Jesus. He cornered anybody who would listen and said, "Hey, remember me? I'm the guy who used to be chained up in the cemetery, crazy as can be with more devils than brains. But look at me now! I'm full of peace and in my right mind. I'm a devil-free zone. All because Jesus Christ of Nazareth, the Son of God, set me free."

Not exactly a glamorous testimony, but who cares? What counts is that it affected the whole city. Because of one man's story, everybody in town heard the gospel. That's what Jesus had in mind all along.

Of course, few of us have a testimony as dramatic as that of Gadara's ex-madman. (Thank heavens.) But it's not the drama that makes the impact. What gets to people is the fact that we have a living Savior who has changed our lives. When we tell them how He loves us and blesses us, they're interested—whether they act like it or not. People are desperate for a God like that.

> IF YOU DON'T KNOW HOW TO TALK TO SOMEONE ABOUT JESUS, JUST TELL HIM WHAT GOD HAS DONE FOR YOU.

The woman at the well in Samaria proved it. She proved you don't need a spine-tingling story to bring people to Jesus. She had no amazing testimony of healing. She hadn't been delivered from demon possession. She didn't even have all her theological ducks in a row. She just had one conversation with Jesus. In that conversation she found out three simple things: that He was the Messiah, that He knew who she was and what she had done, and that He loved her anyway.

What she had to say wasn't half as exciting as what the Gadarene guy had to say. But she was so eager to share it that without even drawing the water she needed from the well,

The woman then left her waterpot, went her way into the city, and said to the men, "Come, see a Man who told me all things that I ever did. Could this be the Christ?" Then they went out of the city and came to Him…And many of the Samaritans of that city believed in Him because of the word of the woman who testified, "He told me all that I ever did." So when the Samaritans had come to Him, they urged Him to stay with them; and He stayed there two days. And many more believed because of His own word. Then they said to the woman, "Now we believe, not because of what you said, for we ourselves have heard Him and we know that this is indeed the Christ, the Savior of the world."

(John 4:28–30, 39–42)

What would have happened if that little lady had let the devil shut her up? What if she'd let him remind her that her five ex-husbands and a live-in boyfriend hadn't exactly earned her a sterling reputation? People already thought she was a little loose. What would they think if she spouted off about seeing the Messiah at the local water well? What would they say if she told them He was so interested in her past that He struck up a conversation with her about it? Why, she'd be the laughingstock of the whole town! Nobody would ever again believe a word she said.

If that woman had entertained such thoughts, Jesus would have waited at the well alone. Nobody would have come out to see Him. And a whole bunch of sad Samaritans would have missed the opportunity to meet their Savior.

Don't let that happen in your life. Don't let the devil convince you that you don't have any interesting stories to tell about your relationship with the Lord. If you know Him at all, you do. Ask Him to remind you of them. Ask Him to help you *"always be ready to give a defense to everyone who asks you a reason for the hope that is in you"* (1 Peter 3:15).

Even if all you have to say is, *I used to be afraid that when I die, I might go to hell. Now I'm not afraid of that anymore. I know I'm going to heaven to spend eternity with Jesus,* that's an awesome testimony. And when people see the peace and joy in you that lets them know you're telling the truth, that testimony will do for them what nothing else can do. It will drop into their hearts and start to sprout.

JR Polhemus can vouch for that. He scoured the whole world—from New York to California and from Ireland to Israel—looking for spiritual truth and came up empty. But when he heard the plain message of the gospel from his old friends, when he looked into their eyes saw in them the life only the Lord can give, he realized his search was over. Like the Samaritans, he said, *"Now I know that this is indeed the Christ, the Savior of the world"* (John 4:42).

If you're concerned that people won't take your word for it when you tell them that Jesus is alive and well, and that He is the Savior of the world, there is something else you can do. You can follow the example of the early believers in the New Testament. You can ask for and expect God to confirm His Word with signs and wonders.

Jesus said He'd do that, you know. After commissioning His disciples to preach the gospel to every creature, He said:

> *These signs will follow those who believe: In My name they will cast out demons; they will speak with new tongues; they will take up serpents; and if they drink anything deadly, it will by no means hurt them; they will lay hands on the sick, and they will recover.* (Mark 16:17–18)

Supernatural signs like healing and miracles are a part of the anointing for salvation. They're supposed to follow every Christian who shares the gospel—normal believers like you and me.

Somewhere along the way the church got confused about that. A rumor got started that only the first apostles or special ministers could expect signs to follow them. Why Christians fell for it, I'll never know. After all, Jesus said as plain as day that these signs will follow *those who believe.* He didn't say, "These signs will follow apostles who believe." He didn't say, "These signs will follow full-time ministers."

Even in the book of Acts, we see believers who weren't a part of the original apostolic group preaching the gospel with signs following. Stephen, for example, wasn't one of those first twelve who followed Jesus. He was what we'd call a layman. He was a deacon who helped with the church food pantry, distributing aid to the poor. Yet Acts 6:8 says that *"Stephen, full of faith and power, did great wonders and signs among the people."* (Maybe someone forgot to tell him that he didn't qualify.)

Stephen wasn't the only one in the New Testament who missed the rumor about signs wonders being reserved for a select few. Other believers as well—people so ordinary they remain unnamed in the Bible—traveled around sharing the gospel, and Acts 11:21 says, *"The hand of the Lord was with them, and a great number believed and turned to the Lord."*

"The hand of the Lord" always refers to the manifested power of God. It speaks of the supernatural work of the Holy Spirit. Acts 4:29–30 tells us that when God stretches out His hand, healings, signs, and wonders take place.

What inspired this group of unknown, ordinary believers to traipse around preaching the gospel and expecting God to confirm it with signs following? The New Testament doesn't tell us, but we can conjecture. We can imagine that they heard reports about the Acts 4 prayer meeting the apostles had. Maybe word got out about how they asked God to stretch forth His hand. Maybe they heard how the building shook in response and decided to pray the same prayer themselves.

Or, maybe they'd just heard that Jesus once promised, *"These signs will follow those who believe"* (Mark 16:17).

One thing's for sure. If the rumor that signs and wonders are reserved for the elite was circulating in those days, they weren't the ones who started it.

GOD WORKS THROUGH ORDINARY BELIEVERS IN EXTRAORDINARY WAYS

"Let me get this straight," you might say. "Are you suggesting God will heal people, drive out demons, and do other supernatural things to confirm the gospel when I share it with someone? Are you saying He'll do that kind of thing for an ordinary believer like me?"

That's exactly what I'm saying. The Bible makes no bones about it, and I'm convinced that if we just pray for God to do it, and act in faith on our prayers by sharing the gospel with more people, we can see miracles happen often in our everyday lives.

My friend Larry Satterlee is one reason I'm so confident about that. The miraculous is almost routine in his life. Signs and wonders have followed him around for years. Although he is a full-time minister now, they began trailing him when he was just another eager believer, excited about sharing the gospel.

Larry has some wonderful real-life, book-of-Acts-type stories. My current favorite is the one he tells about the day some time ago when he took a wrong turn after dropping his granddaughter off at school. He'd intended to drive toward his office but somehow his mind wandered, and he found himself driving back home.

Puzzling over his absentmindedness, he was about to turn around on the street that led to his neighborhood when he noticed a garbage truck rumbling his way. It was still about a quarter-mile away when he spotted it. He had plenty of time to make his turn before it reached the corner. But in his heart he sensed a leading to wait for it to pass.

Oh no, Lord. I don't want to wait. I'll end up driving behind it and those trucks stink! he thought. His protest was to no avail. The leading came again. *Wait!*

Shrugging his shoulders, Larry resigned himself to a smelly drive home.

A few blocks down the road, the drive turned deadly. The rear wheel of the garbage truck clipped a cement curb. Brakes wailed, metal creaked and then screamed against the pavement as the tire blew and the truck careened off the road, crashing through the brush of a nearby field. A cyclone of dust and garbage bits billowed and then settled to the ground.

When Larry reached the truck and looked into the cab to check on the condition of the driver, the seat was empty. The door had been sheered off during the crash. The driver was gone.

Larry glanced around and spotted the man lying with his face buried in a muddy pool of blood about twenty feet away. Kneeling next to the motionless body, he knew that with the mud covering his mouth and clogging his nose, the driver would suffocate soon—if he wasn't dead already. Larry cupped his hands and shoveled the blood-soaked soil away from the driver's face to make room for him to breathe.

He needs air!

Larry stopped digging and stared at the man's back. It was as still and lifeless as the dirt beneath it. He wasn't breathing.

CPR was out of the question. The man's body was so mangled and fragile that it gave way under even a gentle touch. There was only one thing to do.

"Breathe, in Jesus' name!" Larry shouted. "I said, breathe!"

A shudder rippled across the man's shoulder. His back rose, then fell. Larry blinked and looked again to make sure. Once again, he saw the tattered, bloody shirt stretched over the driver's back rise, then fall. The motion was slight but definite. The man was alive.

Seconds later, a passing motorist stopped to help and made a 911 call.

After the garbage truck driver was air-flighted to the hospital, stitched, bandaged, and settled in his hospital bed, one of the first sights he saw was the hulking frame of Larry

Satterlee striding in to visit him. Unsure if the man remembered the scene of the accident, Larry started to explain who he was.

The driver's injuries made it impossible for him to speak, so he grabbed a pen and a notepad and scribbled his message. "I know who you are," he wrote. "And I know what you did. Thank you!"

Over the next few minutes, Larry shared the plan of salvation with him. He told him about Jesus' love and His power to save. The man believed every word. He'd already experienced dramatic evidence of that love and power. He prayed and gave his life to the Lord by writing a prayer on the note pad.

Just as he finished, his wife walked in.

Larry seized the opportunity. "Hello," he said, "Do you want to give your life to Jesus too?"

The woman bristled. "I don't have time to talk about that right now!" she said.

Once again, her husband grabbed the pen and scrawled bold letters on the pad. "You need what this man has!"

Before Larry left the hospital room that day, both the driver and his wife were born again.

That may sound like a once-in-a-lifetime experience. But Larry has had a lot of stories like that. He thinks other believers should too. "*Don't just tell people about the saving power of the Lord Jesus Christ; show them.*" That's what the Lord said to Larry.

If we'd listen, God would say that to the rest of us too.

We don't have to wait for a life-or-death emergency, however, to show off God's saving power. We can do it in everyday situations. A lady I know walked into the dry cleaners one day and noticed the Muslim proprietor nursing his back. When he told her it had been hurting for months, she said, "Jesus can heal that. May I pray for you and ask Him to do it?"

DON'T JUST TELL PEOPLE ABOUT THE SAVING POWER OF THE LORD JESUS CHRIST. SHOW THEM!

The man's pain overcame his Islamic convictions, and he let her pray. When the lady stopped back by a few hours later, the man was healed and more open to the gospel than he'd ever been before.

Another friend of mine was eating lunch in the food court at the mall when the Lord spoke to her about a woman sitting a few tables away from her. "Go tell her that I know about her situation, and I am taking care of it," He said.

It took a few minutes, but my friend eventually overcame her reluctance and obeyed. When she did, the woman burst into tears. The message was just what she needed, and it opened the door for my friend to share the Lord with her.

Those are just a few examples of the supernatural ways God can move through us to release the anointing of salvation. There are other ways He can work as well. First Corinthians 12 tells us about some of them and refers to them as *spiritual gifts* or *manifestations of the Spirit*. It says:

> *Now concerning spiritual gifts, brethren, I do not want you to be ignorant.... There are diversities of gifts, but the same Spirit. There are differences of ministries, but the same Lord. And there are diversities of activities, but it is the same God who works all in all. But the manifestation of the Spirit is given to each one for the profit of all: for to one is given the word of wisdom through the Spirit, to another the word of knowledge through the same Spirit, to another faith by the same Spirit, to another gifts of healings by the same Spirit, to another the working of miracles, to another prophecy, to another discerning of spirits, to another different kinds of tongues, to another the interpretation of tongues. But one and the same Spirit works all these things, distributing to each one individually as He wills.*
>
> (1 Corinthians 12:1, 4–11)

According to those verses, God doesn't work through us all in the same way, but He does work through us all. He gives to each one of us the supernatural gifts we need to reach the people He has called us to reach. He divinely equips us all to bring in our portion of His harvest.

That divine equipping is part of God's anointing for salvation. So go spread the good news and start expecting miracles in your life. Before you head out the door, however, there is one more thing you need to know, one more essential ingredient that must be added to ignite God's explosive, soul-winning power.

DON'T LEAVE HOME WITHOUT IT

Prayer. Nothing in the kingdom of God works without it. It is the bulldozer that shoves the spiritual obstacles aside and prepares the way of the Lord. It is the fuel that propels His Word like a heat-seeking missile into the hearts of the lost and pierces them with the kind of conviction that leaves them crying out for salvation.

Prayer—fervent, heartfelt, believing prayer—brings the fire of the Holy Spirit on the scene and transforms us from lily-livers too timid to publicly declare our faith into lion-hearts who roar the gospel whenever the Lord leads. Jesus considered that Holy Ghost fire so vital that He essentially told the first disciples, "Don't leave home without it."

> He commanded them not to depart from Jerusalem, but to wait for the Promise of the Father, "which," He said, "you have heard from Me; for John truly baptized with water, but you shall be baptized with the Holy Spirit not many days from now...But you shall receive power when the Holy Spirit has come upon you; and you shall be witnesses to Me

154   WILL YOU HOLD OPEN THE DOOR?

*in Jerusalem, and in all Judea and Samaria, and to the end
of the earth."* (Acts 1:4–6, 8)

Peter and the rest of the upper-room crowd knew full well how essential that power would be. Without it, they wouldn't survive a day trying to preach the gospel to the hardheaded, Christ-rejecting neighbors among whom they had been commissioned to build the Jerusalem Community Church. They knew full well that Jesus had given them an impossible task. They had no hope of success at all unless they had God's Holy Spirit, whose power makes all things possible working with them.

So they obeyed Jesus' instructions. They hid away in an upper room in Jerusalem and *"continued with one accord in prayer and supplication"* (verse 14) for ten days. They prayed until the fire fell. They prayed until the Holy Spirit roared into the upper room with a sound that shook Jerusalem like a sonic boom and brought people running from blocks around to see what had happened. They prayed until they praised God with other tongues and declared His Word and didn't care a whit what other people thought about it.

A few days later when the religious leaders threatened to jail them and shut down their revival, they held another prayer meeting. They…

*raised their voice to God with one accord and said: "Lord,
You are God, who made heaven and earth and the sea, and*

all that is in them….Now, Lord, look on their threats, and grant to Your servants that with all boldness they may speak Your word, by stretching out Your hand to heal, and that signs and wonders may be done through the name of Your holy Servant Jesus." And when they had prayed, the place where they were assembled together was shaken; and they were all filled with the Holy Spirit, and they spoke the word of God with boldness. (Acts 4:24, 29–31)

That just goes to show you that it takes more than one prayer meeting to maintain a steady flow of Holy Spirit power. That's why the New Testament tells us to:

- *Watch and pray.* (Matthew 26:41)

- *Always…pray and not lose heart.* (Luke 18:1)

- *Pray without ceasing.* (1 Thessalonians 5:17)

- *Pray everywhere, lifting up holy hands, without wrath and doubting.* (1 Timothy 2:8)

- [Be] *praying always with all prayer and supplication in the Spirit, being watchful to this end with all perseverance and supplication for all the saints.* (Ephesians 6:18)

That's what Mac Gober's grandfather did. He prayed… and prayed…and wouldn't quit. He expected God to do whatever it took to save His grandson. He got what he asked for too—against all natural odds. He proved that if we keep praying for our lost loved ones and refuse to give up, God will send the very lightning of heaven, if necessary, to jolt them into eternal life.

If you don't know how or what to pray for the lost ones you love, you can start by praying what the Bible tells us to. It says:

- We can ask God to send laborers across their path, people specifically anointed reveal to them God's power and touch their hearts. (Matthew 9:37–38)

- We can bind the demonic spirits that have blinded them to the truth of the gospel and pray for God to give them eyes to see. (2 Corinthians 4:4)

- We can ask the Holy Spirit to move upon them in great power and convict them of sin, righteousness, and judgment. (John 16:8)

- We can pray for God to open their hearts, like He opened Lydia's in the book of Acts, to heed the gospel when it is preached to them. (Acts 16:14)

- We can pray for angels to be sent on assignment to help reach them the way they helped reach Cornelius and his household. (Acts 10:3–7)

- We can pray and believe for God to work all kinds of supernatural signs and wonders—to shine lights out of heaven like He did for Saul; to shake walls like He did for the Philippian jailer; to work spectacular miracles that astound our loved ones and turn them to the Lord like He did when He healed the paralyzed man in Lydda and raised Dorcas from the dead in Joppa. (See Acts 9:1–6, 32–42; 16:25–31.)

If we pray those things and still sense there's more spiritual work to do, we can depend on the Holy Spirit to help us get it done. The Bible promises us He will do that, you know. It says He "*helps in our weaknesses. For we do not know what we should pray for as we ought, but the Spirit Himself makes intercession for us with groanings which cannot be uttered. Now He who searches the hearts knows what the mind of the Spirit is, because He makes intercession for the saints according to the will of God*" (Romans 8:26-27).

The Fourth of July All Over Again

Do you know what will happen when we all start praying like that? Do you know what will happen when we hit our knees and ignite the atmosphere once again with God's spiritual fire?

The same kinds of things that happened in the book of Acts.

God will once again lavish His dynamic, miracle-working power upon our lost family members, neighbors, and communities as He did in the days of the early church. He will pour out the supernatural signs and wonders, healings and miracles, soul-cutting conviction, and building-shaking might that we need to win them to Jesus. No longer will we stare in amazement at the events in the book of Acts like kids on the Fourth of July stare at the final burst of fireworks—as if, when the last shining miracle was recorded in the pages of the Bible, the divine sky went dark and the show was over. Instead, we'll be celebrating what God is doing among us right now.

I'm not just saying that because it sounds good. I'm saying that because I believe it—and because I've witnessed book-of-Acts-type miracles myself. I've seen things that made my mind stagger and my knees buckle, wonders that proved God hasn't changed His marketing plan. He still saves souls the same way He did two thousand years ago, when He can find someone who will pray and believe.

The most awesome wonder I've witnessed thus far took place during a believers' meeting in the last week of August 1997 in Birmingham, England. It happened during the altar call. One of the most anointed ministers for evangelism I've ever seen was inviting people to come forward to give their lives to Jesus. At the time, there seemed to be nothing extraordinary about what was happening. It was just an ordinary day at church.

But, as only He can do, God turned the ordinary into the unforgettable in a split second.

"Somebody here has a problem with their eye," the minister said as he scanned the several thousand people in the auditorium. "I saw you in my heart when I was praying before the service, and the Lord told me He was going to heal you."

A hush fell over the crowd and for a moment no one came forward. The minister repeated the offer.

Like everybody else, I turned my head in all directions, watching the aisles to see if anybody would come. After a few seconds, a man emerged from the shadows at the back of the auditorium and loped toward the front. From my vantage point near the center of the front row, I saw him up close as he passed by, and I caught my breath at the sight. His was no minor ailment. The skin around his eye was twisted and disfigured, the tissue a purple-red hue. The eyeball itself had disappeared beneath the whole mess. I couldn't tell if it was painful, but just looking at it made me wince.

He stopped not twenty feet away from me. Whatever was going to happen, I had a front-row seat.

The minister grabbed the man's shoulders and whirled him around so everyone in the meeting could see his condition. "I want you to look at this man!" he shouted, "because in a moment, God is going to heal him!"

Oh, dear heavens! I worried (faith giant that I am). *This could be embarrassing. This isn't a cold or a headache. If God doesn't do a miracle here, we'll all know it.*

Almost before I could finish the thought, the minister spun the man back around and said seven simple words, "Be healed, in the name of Jesus!"

No time passed, it seemed, between those words and the startled yelp of joy that followed them. No time passed, it seemed to me, between the moment I saw the man's eye, twisted and disfigured…and the moment I saw it transformed, whole and perfect.

There was no possible natural explanation for what happened. No one touched him. No abracadabra magic cloth was draped over his head to make way for a sleight of hand trick. The eye just rearranged and became normal under God's invisible hand.

My knees buckled. I've never fainted, but I came close that day. I looked at my friend Terri, who was standing next to me. Her jaw was dangling as low as mine. "Did you see that?" we gasped to each other, our words synchronized.

What happened next was like a scene lifted straight from the pages of Acts. The healed man leaped like a bullfrog to the platform and hopped about, bellowing with glee and shouting praises to God. Another minister who was sitting nearby chased him around for a while with a microphone, trying to get him to stop and tell what the Lord had done for him. When he was able to reach the man and hold him still, his words echoed across the auditorium.

"I was blind!" he cried, "and now I can see!"

I didn't get to talk to the man myself, but if he wasn't born again before that moment, I'd guess he got that way soon afterward. No doubt, so did a lot of other lost people who were standing slack-jawed in the auditorium that day. There's something about coming face-to-face with a miracle. It smashes to bits the arguments of the skeptics. It leaves the intellectuals speechless. It builds a bridge across the chasm of doubt and opens the way for the unbeliever to cross it and reach the firm ground of faith on the other side.

As one of my favorite Bible teachers says, a miracle settles the issue. It ends the dispute and demonstrates that God is real...that Jesus truly is the Savior of mankind, King of kings, and Lord of lords.

If God will work that kind of miracle to win those folks, He will do it to win the loved ones you're praying for. He will put on a display of heavenly power that will shatter the walls of their unbelief and open their hearts like a crocus in spring.

He will release the fullness of His anointing for salvation.

THE ANCIENT SYMBOL THAT NEVER GROWS OLD

BY GINA

THE ANCIENT SYMBOL THAT NEVER GROWS OLD

Anointing oil. If you think it seems oddly out of place on the cover of a contemporary Christian book, you might just be right. In an age where the church is striving above all to be culturally relevant, anointing oil is...well, definitely not that. In fact, most people would say it's just the opposite: a dusty relic from centuries gone by that should be stashed in an attic trunk nestled next to grandmother's dog-eared King James Bible, not perched on the shelves of a popular bookstore.

So why use it? In this day of multi-media savvy readers who pick up prayer alerts on the Internet and download the latest Christian tunes onto their MP3 players, why stick with a symbol so peculiar and old-fashioned?

Because there's no substitute for it.

Anointing oil threads and sparkles its way through the pages of the Bible unlike any other spiritual symbol. From Genesis to the New Testament epistles, it appears again and again, carrying life-changing messages. Spanning not just centuries but millennia, it has proven to be a spiritual picture worth a thousand words.

Although the words *anoint, anointed,* and *anointing* appear more than 150 times in Scripture, and are derived from the Latin word *inunctus,* meaning "smear with oil," anointing oil by itself possesses no mystical properties. It's not magic. It's not even supernatural. Anointing oil cannot heal or deliver or change us at all. The physical application of it alone cannot help us any more than a sermon preached to us in a foreign language. With the oil, as with the sermon, we experience its power only when we understand its message.

What, then, is the message of the anointing oil?

It depends on the situation you're facing.

When it first appears in Genesis 28, anointing oil says God is present. He is here right now to protect and provide for all your needs. At least, that is the essence of its meaning there. To see the fullness of its message, we must read the story that surrounds it.

We must see Jacob—lonely and wandering, banished from home, hated by his brother and haunted by his past, sleeping under the stars with his head resting uneasily on a stony pillow. We must dream with him of a heavenly ladder crowded with angels climbing up and down, bringing to earth the blessings Jacob ached to possess. We must hear God's voice hammering the point home and saying, *"Behold, I am with you and will keep you wherever you go...I will not leave you until I have done what I have spoken to you"* (verse 15).

That night, that dream, and that divine voice changed Jacob's life. He wanted to make sure he never forgot those things. So *"Jacob rose early in the morning, and took the stone that he had put at his head, set it up as a pillar, and poured oil on top of it. And he called the name of the place Bethel"* (verses 18–19).

The Hebrew word *Bethel* means house of God. Think of it! God proved through Jacob's experience that He meets His people in the most stony, desolate seasons of life and pours out His blessings on them. He makes His home with them and promises He will never leave them.

If that had been the only message anointing oil ever preached, the practice of using it would have been worth preserving, but that was just the beginning of what it has to say. In the book of Exodus, anointing oil speaks of holiness and dedication to the Lord. Poured on the priests and splashed around the tabernacle, it declared: *These people and these things belong to God and God alone. They are set apart for His glory.*

In the book of 1 Samuel, the anointing oil says, *This person has been chosen by God to reign as a king.* It takes a simple young shepherd boy named David and marks him as royalty. Dripping onto the ruddy cheeks of the totally unknown and unlikely ruler, it proclaims: *This is the person God will empower to win battles. This is the one who will trample the enemies of the Almighty under his feet.*

In the book of Isaiah, anointing oil preaches a message of deliverance from bondage and freedom from the oppressor. It promises *"that his burden will be taken away from your shoulder, and his yoke from your neck, and the yoke will be destroyed because of the anointing oil"* (Isaiah 10:27).

In 2 Chronicles 28:15, the anointing oil speaks of the refreshing and restoration God provides. In Psalm 23, it assures God's people that God will honor and exalt them before their enemies like an honored guest. In Psalm 105, it proclaims God's fierce and unfailing protection and says of the children of Israel, *"He permitted no one to do them wrong; Yes, He rebuked kings for their sakes, saying, 'Do not touch My anointed ones, and do My prophets no harm'"* (verses 14–15).

ROAD SIGNS TO THE NEW COVENANT

"But those are all Old Testament messages," someone might argue. "Do they really apply to Christians today?"

Yes! In fact, they apply more surely to us than to the people who first received them. *"They were written for our admonition, upon whom the ends of the ages have come"* (1 Corinthians 10:11). Every time anointing oil was used under the old covenant, it pointed forward to the new. Like a sign along the highway, it alerted spiritual travelers to their ultimate destination, to a time when Jesus would open the door for the Holy Spirit to be poured out like anointing oil on all who believed in Him. All through the Old Testament, the anointing oil was preaching about the *Christ*!

Many believers today don't realize it, but the very word *Christ* practically shimmers with anointing oil because it literally means *the anointed one*. No wonder Jesus began His ministry on earth by declaring:

> *The Spirit of the* Lord *is upon Me, because He has anointed Me to preach the gospel to the poor; He has sent Me to heal the brokenhearted, to proclaim liberty to the captives and recovery of sight to the blind, to set at liberty those who are oppressed; to proclaim the acceptable year of the* Lord.
> (Luke 4:18–19)

Every glistening drop of anointing oil administered by believers today speaks about Jesus. It declares that because of the blood He shed and the Holy Spirit He has poured out upon us:

- His presence is here with us and in us, transforming each one of us into little Bethels, mobile dwelling places of God.

- We belong to God and God alone. Like the Old Testament priests and tabernacle, we are set apart for His glory, *"a chosen race, a royal priesthood, a dedicated nation,* [God's] *own, purchased, special people that we may set forth the wonderful deeds and display the virtues and perfections of Him who called us out of darkness into His marvelous light"* (1 Peter 2:9 AMP).
- We have been given the divine authority and power to reign as kings in life through the One Man Jesus Christ (Romans 5:17 AMP).
- We have been freed from the devil's oppression and honored with every spiritual blessing in heavenly places (Ephesians 1:3).
- We are no longer slaves, but more than conquerors through Him who loved us (Romans 8:37).

Those messages are powerful by themselves, yet they are enhanced even further when biblical fragrances are added because each scent symbolizes an aspect of our Savior. The Rose of Sharon scented oil in this book, for example, represents the spiritual salvation He provides us. It reminds us that our heavenly Bridegroom—like the Rose of Sharon bridegroom in Song of Solomon—delivers us from the wilderness of sin and brings us into His garden of righteousness. Such fragrances have special significance for us as the body of Christ today. Paul revealed why in 2 Corinthians 2:11 when he wrote:

But thanks be to God! For through what Christ has done, he has triumphed over us so that now wherever we go he uses us to tell others about the Lord and to spread the Gospel like a sweet perfume. As far as God is concerned there is a sweet, wholesome fragrance in our lives. It is the fragrance of Christ within us, an aroma to both the saved and the unsaved all around us. To those who are not being saved, we seem a fearful smell of death and doom, while to those who know Christ we are a life-giving perfume. (TLB)

In the light of those verses, we see that all the sweet fragrances in the Old Testament point not only to Jesus but to *us*. They also represent our prayers, which Revelation 5:8 tells us are lifted in heaven to God as *"golden bowls full of incense."* What a picture that is: God Almighty breathing into Himself the fragrant prayers of His anointed people, then breathing back out again the answers to those prayers!

That is the picture painted by anointing oil. Once we see it, we can easily understand why the first twelve disciples used that symbol when they ministered to the multitudes in Jesus' name. We can grasp, even with our contemporary Christian minds, why *"they anointed with oil many who were sick, and healed them"* (Mark 6:13).

Suddenly the instructions in James 5:14 no longer sound odd and archaic. *"Is anyone among you sick? Let him call for the elders of the church, and let them pray over him, anointing him with oil in the name of the Lord."* In the light of what that oil has preached to God's people through the ages, it's easy to imagine how the heart of an ailing saint who understood its message might leap with joy as that oil touched his skin. We can almost hear its sermon thundering in his ears, declaring that the burden-removing, yoke-destroying power of Jesus Himself has been released in his body. The One anointed to heal…and deliver…and honor…and protect…and bring victory is here!

That, in essence, is the message of anointing oil. Whether the symbol is culturally relevant may be up for debate. But one thing is indisputable: what it stands for will always be relevant—in every culture, in every age, in every place. For hidden within that simple bottle of oil is the liberating gospel of the Lord Jesus Christ, the message that never grows old.

The Lord is my strength and song, and He has become my salvation; He is my God, and I will praise Him.

(Exodus 15:2)

My heart rejoices in the Lord; my horn is exalted in the Lord. I smile at my enemies, because I rejoice in Your salvation.

(1 Samuel 2:1)

The Lord is my rock, my fortress and my deliverer; the God of my strength, in Him I will trust, my shield and the horn of my salvation. (2 Samuel 22:2–3)

You have also given me the shield of Your salvation, and Your gentleness has made me great. (2 Samuel 22:36)

The Lord lives! Blessed be my Rock! Let God be exalted, the Rock of my salvation! (2 Samuel 22:47)

Although my house is not so with God, yet He has made with me an everlasting covenant, ordered in all things and secure. For this is all my salvation and all my desire; will He not make it increase? (2 Samuel 23:5)

Sing to the Lord, all the earth; proclaim the good news of His salvation from day to day...And say, "Save us, O God of our salvation." (1 Chronicles 16:23, 35)

Let Your priests, O Lord God, be clothed with salvation, and let Your saints rejoice in goodness. (2 Chronicles 6:41)

Salvation belongs to the Lord. Your blessing is upon Your people. (Psalm 3:8)

I will rejoice in Your salvation. (Psalm 9:14)

But I have trusted in Your mercy; my heart shall rejoice in Your salvation. (Psalm 13:5)

The Lord is my rock and my fortress and my deliverer; my God, my strength, in whom I will trust; my shield and the horn of my salvation, my stronghold. (Psalm 18:2)

You have also given me the shield of Your salvation; Your right hand has held me up, Your gentleness has made me great. (Psalm 18:35)

We will rejoice in your salvation, and in the name of our God we will set up our banners! May the Lord fulfill all your petitions. (Psalm 20:5)

Lead me in Your truth and teach me, for You are the God of my salvation; On You I wait all the day. (Psalm 25:5)

And my soul shall be joyful in the Lord; It shall rejoice in His salvation. (Psalm 35:9)

But the salvation of the righteous is from the Lord. (Psalm 37:39)

Make haste to help me, O Lord, my salvation! (Psalm 38:22)

Truly my soul silently waits for God; from Him comes my salvation. He only is my rock and my salvation…In God is my salvation and my glory. (Psalm 62:1–2, 7)

God be merciful to us and bless us, And cause His face to shine upon us. Selah. That Your way may be known on earth, Your salvation among all nations. (Psalm 67:1–2)

Blessed be the Lord, Who daily loads us with benefits, the God of our salvation! (Psalm 68:19)

My mouth shall tell of Your righteousness and Your salvation all the day. (Psalm 71:15)

For God is my King from of old, working salvation in the midst of the earth. (Psalm 74:12)

Restore us, O God of our salvation, and cause Your anger toward us to cease. (Psalm 85:4)

Show us Your mercy, O Lord, and grant us Your salvation. (Psalm 85:7)

Surely His salvation is near to those who fear Him. (Psalm 85:9)

Sing to the Lord, bless His name; proclaim the good news of His salvation from day to day. (Psalm 96:2)

The Lord has made known His salvation; His righteousness He has openly shown in the sight of the nations. (Psalm 98:2)

Remember me, O Lord, with the favor You have toward Your people; Oh, visit me with Your salvation. (Psalm 106:4)

I will take up the cup of salvation, and call upon the name of the Lord. (Psalm 116:13)

The Lord is my strength and song, and He has become my salvation. The voice of rejoicing and salvation is in the tents of the righteous. (Psalm 118:14–15)

I will praise You, for You have answered me, and have become my salvation. (Psalm 118:21)

Let Your mercies come also to me, O Lord Your salvation according to Your word. (Psalm 119:41)

My soul faints for Your salvation, but I hope in Your word. (Psalm 119:81)

For the Lord takes pleasure in His people; He will beautify the humble with salvation. (Psalm 149:4)

Behold, God is my salvation, I will trust and not be afraid; "For YAH, the Lord, is my strength and my song; He also has become my salvation." Therefore with joy you will draw water from the wells of salvation. (Isaiah 12:2–3)

This is the Lord; we have waited for Him; we will be glad and rejoice in His salvation. (Isaiah 25:9)

Rain down, you heavens, from above, and let the skies pour down righteousness; let the earth open, let them bring forth salvation, and let righteousness spring up together.

(Isaiah 45:8)

I bring My righteousness near, it shall not be far off; My salvation shall not linger. (Isaiah 46:13)

Thus says the Lord: "In an acceptable time I have heard You, and in the day of salvation I have helped You; I will preserve You and give You as a covenant to the people, to restore the earth, to cause them to inherit the desolate heritages." (Isaiah 49:8)

How beautiful upon the mountains are the feet of him who brings good news, who proclaims peace, who brings glad tidings of good things, who proclaims salvation, who says to Zion, "Your God reigns!" (Isaiah 52:7)

He saw that there was no man, and wondered that there was no intercessor; therefore His own arm brought salvation for Him. (Isaiah 59:16)

I will greatly rejoice in the Lord, my soul shall be joyful in my God; for He has clothed me with the garments of salvation, He has covered me with the robe of righteousness, as a bridegroom decks himself with ornaments, and as a bride adorns herself with her jewels. (Isaiah 61:10)

Surely your salvation is coming. (Isaiah 62:11)

You went forth for the salvation of Your people, for salvation with Your Anointed. (Habakkuk 3:13)

When His disciples heard it, they were exceedingly amazed, saying, "Who then can be saved?" But Jesus looked at them and said to them, "With men this is impossible, but with God all things are possible." (Matthew 19:25–26)

And Jesus came and spoke to them, saying, "All authority has been given to Me in heaven and on earth. "Go therefore and make disciples of all the nations, baptizing them in the name of the Father and of the Son and of the Holy Spirit, teaching them to observe all things that I have commanded you; and lo, I am with you always, even to the end of the age." Amen. (Matthew 28:18–20)

And He said to them, "Go into all the world and preach the gospel to every creature. He who believes and is baptized will be saved; but he who does not believe will be condemned. And these signs will follow those who believe: In My name they will cast out demons; they will speak with new tongues; they will take up serpents; and if they drink anything deadly, it will by no means hurt them; they will lay hands on the sick, and they will recover." (Mark 16:15–18)

Blessed is the Lord God of Israel, for He has visited and redeemed His people, and has raised up a horn of salvation. (Luke 1:68–69)

For you will go before the face of the Lord to prepare His ways, to give knowledge of salvation to His people by the remission of their sins. (Luke 1:76–77)

Every valley shall be filled and every mountain and hill brought low; and the crooked places shall be made straight and the rough ways made smooth; and all flesh shall see the salvation of God. (Luke 3:5–6)

Then He said to the woman, "Your faith has saved you. Go in peace." (Luke 7:50)

And Jesus said to him, "Today salvation has come to this house, because he also is a son of Abraham; for the Son of Man has come to seek and to save that which was lost." (Luke 19:9–10)

For God so loved the world that He gave His only begotten Son, that whoever believes in Him should not perish but have everlasting life. For God did not send His Son into the world to condemn the world, but that the world through Him might be saved. (John 3:16–17)

I am the door. If anyone enters by Me, he will be saved, and will go in and out and find pasture. (John 10:9)

And it shall come to pass that whoever calls on the name of the Lord shall be saved. (Acts 2:21)

And with many other words he testified and exhorted them, saying, "Be saved from this perverse generation." Then those who gladly received his word were baptized; and that day about three thousand souls were added to them…And the Lord added to the church daily those who were being saved. (Acts 2:40–41, 47)

But those things which God foretold by the mouth of all His prophets, that the Christ would suffer, He has thus fulfilled.

Repent therefore and be converted, that your sins may be blotted out, so that times of refreshing may come from the presence of the Lord. (Acts 3:18–19)

Many of those who heard the word believed; and the number of the men came to be about five thousand. (Acts 4:4)

Nor is there salvation in any other, for there is no other name under heaven given among men by which we must be saved. (Acts 4:12)

Then the word of God spread, and the number of the disciples multiplied greatly in Jerusalem, and a great many of the priests were obedient to the faith. (Acts 6:7)

Then Philip went down to the city of Samaria and preached Christ to them. And the multitudes with one accord heeded the things spoken by Philip, hearing and seeing the miracles which he did. For unclean spirits, crying with a loud voice, came out of many who were possessed; and many who were paralyzed and lame were healed. And there was great joy in that city. (Acts 8:5–8)

Now it came to pass, as Peter went through all parts of the country, that he also came down to the saints who dwelt in Lydda. There he found a certain man named Aeneas, who had been bedridden eight years and was paralyzed. And Peter said to him, "Aeneas, Jesus the Christ heals you. Arise and make your bed." Then he arose immediately. So all who dwelt at Lydda and Sharon saw him and turned to the Lord. (Acts 9:32–35)

To you the word of this salvation has been sent. And we declare to you glad tidings; that promise which was made to the fathers. God has fulfilled this for us their children, in that He has raised up Jesus. As it is also written in the second Psalm: "You are My Son, Today I have begotten You." And that He raised Him from the dead, no more to return to corruption…Therefore let it be known to you, brethren, that through this Man is preached to you the forgiveness of sins; and by Him everyone who believes is justified from all things from which you could not be justified by the law of Moses.   (Acts 13:26, 32–34, 38–39)

And he brought them out and said, "Sirs, what must I do to be saved?" So they said, "Believe on the Lord Jesus Christ, and you will be saved, you and your household."

(Acts 16:31)

Therefore let it be known to you that the salvation of God has been sent to the Gentiles, and they will hear it!

(Acts 28:29)

For I am not ashamed of the gospel of Christ, for it is the power of God to salvation for everyone who believes.

(Romans 1:16)

But God demonstrates His own love toward us, in that while we were still sinners, Christ died for us. Much more then, having now been justified by His blood, we shall be saved from wrath through Him.   (Romans 5:8–9)

For if when we were enemies we were reconciled to God through the death of His Son, much more, having been reconciled, we shall be saved by His life. And not only that, but we also rejoice in God through our Lord Jesus Christ, through whom we have now received the reconciliation.

(Romans 5:10–11)

But what does it say? "The word is near you, even in your mouth and in your heart" (that is, the word of faith which we preach): that if you confess with your mouth the Lord Jesus and believe in your heart that God has raised Him from the dead, you will be saved. For with the heart one believes to righteousness, and with the mouth confession is made to salvation. (Romans 10:8–10)

For "whoever calls upon the name of the Lord shall be saved." (Romans 10:13)

For the message of the cross is foolishness to those who are perishing, but to us who are being saved it is the power of God. (1 Corinthians 1:18)

For He says: "In an acceptable time I have heard you, and in the day of salvation I have helped you." Behold, now is the accepted time; behold, now is the day of salvation.

(2 Corinthians 6:2)

For godly sorrow produces repentance to salvation.

(2 Corinthians 7:10)

In Him you also trusted, after you heard the word of truth, the gospel of your salvation; in whom also, having believed, you were sealed with the Holy Spirit of promise, who is the guarantee of our inheritance until the redemption of the purchased possession, to the praise of His glory.

(Ephesians 1:13–14)

But God, who is rich in mercy, because of His great love with which He loved us, even when we were dead in trespasses, made us alive together with Christ (by grace you have been saved). (Ephesians 2:4–5)

For by grace you have been saved through faith, and that not of yourselves; it is the gift of God, not of works, lest anyone should boast. (Ephesians 2:8–9)

But let us who are of the day be sober, putting on the breastplate of faith and love, and as a helmet the hope of salvation. For God did not appoint us to wrath, but to obtain salvation through our Lord Jesus Christ, who died for us, that whether we wake or sleep, we should live together with Him.

(1 Thessalonians 5:8–10)

But we are bound to give thanks to God always for you, brethren beloved by the Lord, because God from the beginning chose you for salvation through sanctification by the Spirit and belief in the truth, to which He called you by our gospel, for the obtaining of the glory of our Lord Jesus Christ. (2 Thessalonians 2:13–14)

For this is good and acceptable in the sight of God our Savior, who desires all men to be saved and to come to the knowledge of the truth. (1 Timothy 2:3–4)

Therefore do not be ashamed of the testimony of our Lord, nor of me His prisoner, but share with me in the sufferings for the gospel according to the power of God, who has saved us and called us with a holy calling, not according to our works, but according to His own purpose and grace which was given to us in Christ Jesus before time began.
(2 Timothy 1:8–9)

Therefore I endure all things for the sake of the elect, that they also may obtain the salvation which is in Christ Jesus with eternal glory. (2 Timothy 2:10)

But as for you, continue in the things which you have learned and been assured of, knowing from whom you have learned them, and that from childhood you have known the Holy Scriptures, which are able to make you wise for salvation through faith which is in Christ Jesus. (2 Timothy 3:14–15)

For the grace of God that brings salvation has appeared to all men. (Titus 2:11)

But when the kindness and the love of God our Savior toward man appeared, not by works of righteousness which we have done, but according to His mercy He saved us, through the washing of regeneration and renewing of the Holy Spirit, whom He poured out on us abundantly through Jesus Christ our Savior. (Titus 3:4–6)

And having been perfected, He became the author of eternal salvation to all who obey Him. (Hebrews 5:9)

And as it is appointed for men to die once, but after this the judgment, so Christ was offered once to bear the sins of many. To those who eagerly wait for Him He will appear a second time, apart from sin, for salvation.

(Hebrews 9:27–28)

Blessed be the God and Father of our Lord Jesus Christ, who according to His abundant mercy has begotten us again to a living hope through the resurrection of Jesus Christ from the dead, to an inheritance incorruptible and undefiled and that does not fade away, reserved in heaven for you, who are kept by the power of God through faith for salvation ready to be revealed in the last time. (1 Peter 1:3–5)

Though now you do not see Him, yet believing, you rejoice with joy inexpressible and full of glory, receiving the end of your faith the salvation of your souls. (1 Peter 1:8–9)

For whatever is born of God overcomes the world. And this is the victory that has overcome the world; our faith. Who is he who overcomes the world, but he who believes that Jesus is the Son of God? (1 John 5:4–5)

And this is the testimony: that God has given us eternal life, and this life is in His Son. He who has the Son has life; he who does not have the Son of God does not have life.

(1 John 5:11–12)

Salvation belongs to our God who sits on the throne, and to the Lamb! (Revelation 7:10)

Now salvation, and strength, and the kingdom of our God, and the power of His Christ have come. (Revelation 12:10)

SCRIPTURES FOR SALVATION

ABOUT THE
AUTHORS

About the Authors

Melanie Hemry

A former intensive care nurse, Melanie Hemry traded in her stethoscope for a computer and now writes poignant true life stories, many of which are set in intensive care. A winner of the coveted *Guideposts* Writing Contest, Melanie's stories have warmed the hearts of readers around the world. She holds a bachelor of science in nursing from the University of Central Oklahoma and a master's degree in Practical Ministry from Wagner Leadership Institute in Colorado Springs. Melanie is also the author of *A Healing Touch: The Power of Prayer.*

She can be reached at melaniehemry.com.

About the Authors

Gina Lynnes

A writer by trade and a minister at heart, Gina Lynnes has been a Bible teacher and associate pastor since 1996, ministering especially on the subject of prayer in churches both in the Unites States and abroad. A recipient of the National Religious Broadcasters award for her writing of the *UpReach!* Radio broadcast, she has been involved in Christian publishing for more than twenty years, working behind the scenes as a writer and editor for a number of international ministries. Gina and her husband founded Lynnes Ministries in 2001, and spend their time ministering in Colorado, where they now reside, and in churches across the country.

She can be reached at lynnesministries.com.

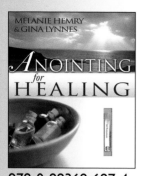
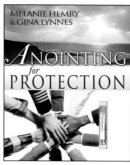
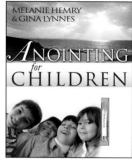

978-0-88368-687-4
176 pages

978-0-88368-689-8
208 pages

978-0-88368-686-7
192 pages

Anointing oil. There's no substitute for it. Hidden within that simple bottle of oil is the liberating gospel of the Lord Jesus Christ, the message that never grows old. In these gift books, each with a 1 mL bottle of scented oil, Melanie Hemry and Gina Lynnes share miraculous stories and personal triumphs that will inspire your faith. *Anointing for Healing* provides faith-building, scriptural instruction for anyone who wants to receive a miracle from the hand of God. *Anointing for Protection* shows how you can live in supernatural security even in the most dangerous of times. Whether you're hoping to have a baby, needing healing for your child, or praying for a prodigal to come home, *Anointing for Children* has a message of hope and faith for you.

WHITAKER HOUSE

www.whitakerhouse.com